OPPOSING
VIEWPOINTS®
SERIES

# Church and State

# Other Books of Related Interest:

## At Issue Series

Should Religious Symbols Be Allowed on Public Land?

What Rights Should Illegal Immigrants Have?

## Global Viewpoints Series

Democracy

Human Rights

## Introducing Issues with Opposing Viewpoints Series

Civil Liberties

Gay Marriage

## Opposing Viewpoints Series

The Catholic Church

Gays in the Military

Illegal Immigration

Presidential Powers

Religion in America

"Congress shall make no law ... abridging the freedom of speech, or of the press."

*First Amendment to the US Constitution*

The basic foundation of our democracy is the First Amendment guarantee of freedom of expression. The Opposing Viewpoints Series is dedicated to the concept of this basic freedom and the idea that it is more important to practice it than to enshrine it.

# Church and State

*Lynn M. Zott, Book Editor*

**GREENHAVEN PRESS**
*A part of Gale, Cengage Learning*

Detroit • New York • San Francisco • New Haven, Conn • Waterville, Maine • London

Elizabeth Des Chenes, *Managing Editor*

© 2012 Greenhaven Press, a part of Gale, Cengage Learning

Gale and Greenhaven Press are registered trademarks used herein under license.

*For more information, contact:*
Greenhaven Press
27500 Drake Rd.
Farmington Hills, MI 48331-3535
Or you can visit our Internet site at gale.cengage.com

For product information and technology assistance, contact us at

Gale Customer Support, 1-800-877-4253
For permission to use material from this text or product, submit all requests online at www.cengage.com/permissions

Further permissions questions can be emailed to permissionrequest@cengage.com

Articles in Greenhaven Press anthologies are often edited for length to meet page requirements. In addition, original titles of these works are changed to clearly present the main thesis and to explicitly indicate the author's opinion. Every effort is made to ensure that Greenhaven Press accurately reflects the original intent of the authors. Every effort has been made to trace the owners of copyrighted material.

Cover image © Bob Daemmrich/Corbis.

**LIBRARY OF CONGRESS CATALOGING-IN-PUBLICATION DATA**

Church and state / Lynn M. Zott, book editor.
    p. cm. -- (Opposing viewpoints)
    Includes bibliographical references and index.
    ISBN 978-0-7377-5432-2 (hardcover) -- ISBN 978-0-7377-5433-9 (pbk.)
    1. Church and state--United States. I. Zott, Lynn M. (Lynn Marie), 1969-
    BR526.C4698 2011
    322'.10973--dc22
                                                              2011008702

Printed in the United States of America
1 2 3 4 5 6 7 15 14 13 12 11

# Contents

# Chapter 4: How Does the Separation of Church and State Affect Other Issues?

# Why Consider Opposing Viewpoints?

> *"The only way in which a human being can make some approach to knowing the whole of a subject is by hearing what can be said about it by persons of every variety of opinion and studying all modes in which it can be looked at by every character of mind. No wise man ever acquired his wisdom in any mode but this."*
>
> *John Stuart Mill*

In our media-intensive culture it is not difficult to find differing opinions. Thousands of newspapers and magazines and dozens of radio and television talk shows resound with differing points of view. The difficulty lies in deciding which opinion to agree with and which "experts" seem the most credible. The more inundated we become with differing opinions and claims, the more essential it is to hone critical reading and thinking skills to evaluate these ideas. Opposing Viewpoints books address this problem directly by presenting stimulating debates that can be used to enhance and teach these skills. The varied opinions contained in each book examine many different aspects of a single issue. While examining these conveniently edited opposing views, readers can develop critical thinking skills such as the ability to compare and contrast authors' credibility, facts, argumentation styles, use of persuasive techniques, and other stylistic tools. In short, the Opposing Viewpoints Series is an ideal way to attain the higher-level thinking and reading skills so essential in a culture of diverse and contradictory opinions.

In addition to providing a tool for critical thinking, Opposing Viewpoints books challenge readers to question their own strongly held opinions and assumptions. Most people form their opinions on the basis of upbringing, peer pressure, and personal, cultural, or professional bias. By reading carefully balanced opposing views, readers must directly confront new ideas as well as the opinions of those with whom they disagree. This is not to simplistically argue that everyone who reads opposing views will—or should—change his or her opinion. Instead, the series enhances readers' understanding of their own views by encouraging confrontation with opposing ideas. Careful examination of others' views can lead to the readers' understanding of the logical inconsistencies in their own opinions, perspective on why they hold an opinion, and the consideration of the possibility that their opinion requires further evaluation.

## Evaluating Other Opinions

To ensure that this type of examination occurs, Opposing Viewpoints books present all types of opinions. Prominent spokespeople on different sides of each issue as well as well-known professionals from many disciplines challenge the reader. An additional goal of the series is to provide a forum for other, less known, or even unpopular viewpoints. The opinion of an ordinary person who has had to make the decision to cut off life support from a terminally ill relative, for example, may be just as valuable and provide just as much insight as a medical ethicist's professional opinion. The editors have two additional purposes in including these less known views. One, the editors encourage readers to respect others' opinions—even when not enhanced by professional credibility. It is only by reading or listening to and objectively evaluating others' ideas that one can determine whether they are worthy of consideration. Two, the inclusion of such viewpoints encourages the important critical thinking skill of objectively evaluating an author's credentials and bias. This evaluation will illuminate an author's reasons for taking a particular stance on an issue and will aid in readers' evaluation of the author's ideas.

It is our hope that these books will give readers a deeper understanding of the issues debated and an appreciation of the complexity of even seemingly simple issues when good and honest people disagree. This awareness is particularly important in a democratic society such as ours in which people enter into public debate to determine the common good. Those with whom one disagrees should not be regarded as enemies but rather as people whose views deserve careful examination and may shed light on one's own.

Thomas Jefferson once said that "difference of opinion leads to inquiry, and inquiry to truth." Jefferson, a broadly educated man, argued that "if a nation expects to be ignorant and free . . . it expects what never was and never will be." As individuals and as a nation, it is imperative that we consider the opinions of others and examine them with skill and discernment. The Opposing Viewpoints Series is intended to help readers achieve this goal.

*David L. Bender and Bruno Leone,*
*Founders*

# Introduction

> "Our Founders understood that the best way to honor the place of faith in the lives of our people was to protect their freedom to practice religion."
>
> —Barack Obama

In December 2009, *The New York Times* published a story about a proposed Islamic community center planned to be built a few blocks away from the World Trade Center site, also known as Ground Zero. The World Trade Center site is notorious as the location of the September 11, 2001, terrorist attacks, when radical al Qaeda terrorists crashed two planes, one each into the north and south towers of the World Trade Center, killing nearly three thousand people. Initially, the story of the proposed community center, originally called Cordoba House and then the Park51 project, attracted little attention. After all, the location was already being used for Muslim worship along with other mosques in the area, and Manhattan is a diverse borough with people of all faiths working and living side by side.

In May 2010 plans for the thirteen-floor community center were reviewed by the local community board in lower Manhattan. Those plans included a five-hundred-seat auditorium, theater, a performing arts center, a swimming pool, a gym, basketball court, a bookstore, an art studio, a child-care center, a cooking school, a food court, and a memorial to the victims of the September 11 attacks. The center also would have prayer space for approximately one to two thousand Muslim worshippers. The proposed project was conceived to be a meeting place for the community, where different faiths could come together for lectures, classes, group discussions, seminars, sports, movies, and other activities. In the words of the project's organizers, it was intended to be "a platform for multi-faith dialogue. It will strive to promote inter-community peace, tolerance and understanding locally in New York City, nationally in America, and globally."

Around the time the plans were being reviewed by the local community board, the media began to publicize the project. Conservative bloggers sparked a national controversy, calling the project the "Ground Zero mosque" and accusing proponents of the project of being insensitive to the families of 9/11 victims. Critics argued that because the terrorists were Muslim, a mosque so close to the World Trade Center site would be a grating and heartbreaking reminder of the losses suffered by the 9/11 victims and their families. Some opponents of the project went even further, accusing the group behind it of erecting a "victory memorial" to Islam.

The Cordoba House project became a national controversy. Pundits from both ends of the political spectrum weighed in, and the debate raged on television, radio, and the Internet. Americans had strong feelings about the issue, and polls reported that most Americans opposed it.

With such fevered opposition, the arguments against the project escalated even further. Opponents accused Imam Feisal Abdul Rauf, chairman of the Cordoba Movement and organizer of the project, of taking money from Islamic radicals and demanded a thorough investigation of the project's funding. Others tried to have the building, a former retail store, designated a landmark so the project's organizers could not tear it down. Carl Paladino, the 2010 Republican candidate for governor of New York, proclaimed that if elected, he would use eminent domain to take over the site and make it a war memorial "instead of a monument to those who attacked our country."

Supporters of the project argued that such actions were based on religious intolerance and were a violation of the

First Amendment of the US Constitution, which assures all Americans of the right to religious freedom. Project supporters pointed out that the building is private property, and the owners have the right to use it as a house of worship.

At the height of the controversy in August 2010, New York City mayor Michael Bloomberg gave a speech about the project, viewing it as a crucial test of church-state separation. "The government has no right whatsoever to deny that right—and if it were tried, the courts would almost certainly strike it down as a violation of the U.S. Constitution," he observed. "Whatever you may think of the proposed mosque and community center, lost in the heat of the debate has been a basic question—should government attempt to deny private citizens the right to build a house of worship on private property based on their particular religion? That may happen in other countries, but we should never allow it to happen here. This nation was founded on the principle that the government must never choose between religions, or favor one over another. . . . For that reason, I believe that this is an important test of the separation of church and state—as important a test as we may see in our lifetimes—and it is critically important that we get it right." In July 2011, the New York Supreme Court ruled that the Muslim facility could begin building, yet the debate surrounding the issue will no doubt continue.

The authors of the viewpoints presented in *Opposing Viewpoints: Church and State* explore the principle of church-state separation in the following chapters: What Should Be the Relationship Between Church and State in the United States? How Does the Wall Between Church and State Affect Political Issues? How Does the Separation of Church and State Impact Policy Decisions? and How Does the Separation of Church and State Affect Other Issues? The information in this volume will provide insight into the often contentious relationship between religious expression and public and political life in the

United States, as the authors debate how the wall of separation between church and state has affected a number of policy decisions in recent years.

CHAPTER 1

# What Should the Relationship Be Between Church and State in the US?

# Chapter Preface

In recent years, the historical and constitutional basis for the concept of the separation between church and state in American life has come under fire from those striving for greater religious expression in the public square and in the political arena. Advocates for greater religious expression point out that the words "separation of church and state" and "wall between church and state" are not in the US Constitution, therefore the nation's Founding Fathers did not intend for there to be such a separation. In fact, they argue, there is plenty of evidence to show that America was built on Christian principles and values and should be considered a Christian nation. In our modern world, that means that religious expression—such as school prayer and the teaching of creationism in schools—should be permitted and churches should be allowed to express political viewpoints without criticism or censure.

Opponents of this view contend that although the specific phrase "separation of church and state" is not in the First Amendment of the Constitution, the principle of separation is at the very heart of the establishment clause, which states that "Congress shall make no law respecting an establishment of religion." They further argue that by preventing Congress from making any law that would establish religion, the nation's founders intended to build a wall between government and religion. This wall would protect not only religions from interference by the government, but the government from interference from religion.

The actual phrase "separation of church and state" did not appear until January 1, 1802, when President Thomas Jefferson sent a letter to the Danbury Baptist Association of Connecticut. At that time, the Baptists were feeling threatened by the state, and they wrote to Jefferson to express their fear that they were being targeted because of their religious views. In his response, Jefferson assured them that they would not be targeted, referring to a "a wall of separation between church and state" that guaranteed their religious freedom in America.

The courts did not get a chance to weigh in on the issue until the 1947 Supreme Court case *Everson v. Board of Education*, which involved the constitutionality of a New Jersey law allowing school districts to arrange daily transportation for children to religious school. The plaintiff, Arch Everson, filed a lawsuit arguing that reimbursements for children attending private religious schools violated the constitutional prohibition against state support of religion and the Constitution's due process clause. The Supreme Court justices were divided about whether the New Jersey policy constituted support of religion but decided that the practice did not violate the Constitution. In their opinions, however, they firmly established that there must be a strong separation between government and religion. The court's *Everson* ruling stated:

> The establishment of religion clause means at least this: Neither a state nor the federal government may set up a church. Neither can pass laws that aid one religion, aid all religions, or prefer one religion over another. Neither can force a person to go to or to remain away from church against his will or force him to profess a belief or disbelief in any religion. . . . Neither a state nor the federal government may, openly or secretly, participate in the affairs of any religious organizations or groups and vice versa. In the words of Jefferson, the clause against establishment of religion by law was intended to erect "a wall of separation between church and state."

With that opinion, the Supreme Court defined the First Amendment religious clause as "a wall of separation between church and state," a precedent that has impacted religious expression in America ever since. Opponents of the decision have continued to try to chip away at the decision and have stressed their interpretation of the First Amendment over the court's decision. It is a debate that goes back to the founding of the United States and will continue to be at the heart of American religious, civic, and political life for years to come.

The historical basis for the separation of church and state is just one of the topics discussed in the following chapter. Other topics include the questions of whether America is a Christian nation and whether religious expression in the United States is too public and political.

*"While it's true that the words 'separa-*
*tion of church and state' are not in the*
*First Amendment, the principle of sepa-*
*ration is at the very heart of the estab-*
*lishment clause."*

# Historically There Has Been a Wall Between Church and State

*Charles C. Haynes*

*Charles C. Haynes is an author and serves as director of the Re-*
*ligious Freedom Education Project at the Newseum in Washing-*
*ton, D.C. In the following viewpoint, he notes that the principle*
*of church-state separation has been under attack in recent years*
*from religious groups that want more political power and influ-*
*ence on policy making. Haynes traces the strong historical prece-*
*dent for the wall between church and state to the establishment*
*clause of the First Amendment, and he asserts that the separa-*
*tion is vital to American religious freedom.*

As you read, consider the following questions:

1. What, according to the author, was the recent conflict concerning the social studies curriculum in Texas?

2. According to Haynes, did the nation's Founding Fathers agree on the application of the separation of church and state?

3. What was James Madison's view on the separation of church and state, as stated by the author?

Not so very long ago, "separation of church and state" was as American as motherhood and apple pie. Despite perennial debates over the degree of separation, public support for the principle itself has been strong for much of our history.

But in today's culture-war climate, the very mention of "separation of church and state" is enough to trigger a bitter argument over the relationship of government and religion in the United States.

## An Epic Battle in Texas

Consider the current fight over the social studies curriculum in Texas. For months now the Democratic minority on the State Board of Education has been sparring with the Republican majority (mostly social conservatives) over what to teach students about the establishment clause of the First Amendment.

The board recently voted down a Democratic proposal calling for students to examine the reasons the Founding Fathers "protected religious freedom in America by barring government from promoting or disfavoring any particular religion over all others"—arguably the mildest possible definition of the "no establishment" mandated by the First Amendment.

A conservative member of the board wants instead for students to "contrast the Founders' intent relative to the wording of the First Amendment's Establishment Clause and Free Exercise Clause, with the popular term 'Separation of church and state.'"

The tug-of-war in Texas over what students should learn about the First Amendment is the latest chapter in a decades-long crusade by some Christian conservatives to denigrate "separation of church and state" as an invention of the courts that ignores the intent of the Founders to create a Christian nation. The phrase, they argue, doesn't appear anywhere in the Constitution.

## Drawn from Historical Precedent

While it's true that the words "separation of church and state" are not in the First Amendment, the principle of separation is at the very heart of the establishment clause. By barring Congress from enacting any law that would have anything to do with an establishment of religion, the Founders clearly intended to keep the federal government, at least, out of the religion business. If that isn't "separation," what is?

That doesn't mean, of course, that the Founders agreed on the application of separation—any more than Americans agree about what separation should look like today. Some voted for the establishment clause to keep the federal government from interfering with state establishments (where, as in Massachusetts and Connecticut, state funds supported favored religious sects).

Others, including James Madison, the primary drafter of the Bill of Rights, supported full disestablishment on all levels of government, arguing that entanglement of church and state had been a leading source of persecution and coercion throughout history.

Madison settled for half a loaf in 1789, when Congress passed the First Amendment, although the church-state separation he argued for was accomplished in all states by 1833. His vision for religious freedom under the federal Constitution wasn't fully realized until the 20th century when the Supreme Court applied the establishment clause to all levels of government through the 14th Amendment [which concerns citizenship and civil rights].

## Tracing the Idea Through History

Ironically, many of the evangelical Christian opponents of separation in Texas today belong to religious groups that were once among the strongest defenders of a high and impregnable wall of separation between church and state. Protestant dissenters in Virginia, for example, were the ground forces in the successful political battle to pass Thomas Jefferson's Statute for Religious Freedom in 1786—the first time in history a legislature voted to separate church from state.

In the 19th and early 20th centuries, many Protestants waved the banner of church-state separation in their crusade to contain the influence of the Roman Catholic Church in America. As late as 1960, presidential candidate John F. Kennedy, a Catholic, felt compelled to travel to Houston to convince a roomful of Protestant ministers that he was fully committed to the "separation of church and state."

The story of Kennedy's religious test is a reminder that the principle of church-state separation has a checkered history—a history that gives the establishment clause a bad name in some quarters.

## A Vital Principle

Attacks on Catholics in the name of "separation of church and state" were unfair and unjust. And contemporary attempts to exclude religion from public life in the name of "separation" are also unfair and unjust.

But abuses of the principle, past and present, should not obscure the vital importance of church-state separation for religious freedom.

What students in Texas (and everywhere else) need to learn is that by separating church from state, the First Amendment protects the independence and integrity of both religion and government—thereby guaranteeing liberty of conscience for us all. [*Editor's note: After this column was written, the Texas State Board of Education adopted new social studies guidelines for the state's schools, including the requirement that students be taught that the words "separation of church and state" are not in the US Constitution.*]

"America got along just fine without this wall for 158 years. . . . It's only been in recent years that it has been twisted into a secularizing influence in our society."

# There Is No Historical Basis for a Separation Between Church and State

*Ken Klukowski*

*Ken Klukowski is special counsel for the Family Research Council. In the following viewpoint, he points out that the "wall of separation between church and state" does not appear anywhere in the US Constitution—and, in fact, the original intent of the so-called establishment clause was to protect religious groups from the state. Klukowski argues that the principle of church-state separation gradually has become twisted to silence people of faith and to lessen their political influence in America.*

As you read, consider the following questions:

1. Which Founding Father was the first to mention the term "wall of separation between church and state," according to the author?

Ken Klukowski, "Perspective: Debating Church and State in Texas," FRC.org, May 24, 2010. Copyright © 2010 by Family Research Council. Reproduced by permission.

2. As stated by Klukowski, when does the "wall of separation between church and state" appear in American law?

3. How did the Supreme Court clarify the principle of church-state separation in 1952, as explained by the author?

A battle is raging in Texas over our children's minds. One of the focal points is the "wall of separation" between church and state. It's a wall based on a false assumption, one that has distorted religious freedom in this country.

The Texas Board of Education must approve textbooks taught in Texan public schools. Its members are the gatekeepers who determine whether a textbook meets curriculum requirements. That board recently met to approve the next generation of books.

But as goes Texas, so goes the nation, because Texan standards are then adopted for textbooks sold all over America. So publishers take drafts to Texas for consultation and approval, making changes as necessary.

One of the changes that conservatives are pushing is for these textbooks to include a discussion of the "wall of separation between church and state." More specifically, they are pushing for a discussion of what the Founding Fathers thought of this wall.

That is a worthwhile classroom discussion, because the Founding Fathers never created such a wall. That's why it's not mentioned in the Constitution.

## The Origins of the "Wall"

On January 1, 1802, President Thomas Jefferson sent a letter to the Danbury Baptists of Connecticut, in response to their congratulations upon his winning the presidency. In it, Jefferson referred to a "wall of separation between church and state." He wrote this in the context of perceived threats the Baptists felt were coming from the state, not the other way around.

After writing that letter, Jefferson went on attending church, at services held in the House chamber of the U.S. Congress. (On Sundays, the Capitol was a church building.) He also went on to approve legislation for the federal government to undertake the construction of churches in the frontier regions, and helping pay pastors to preach in these churches, to carry the Christian faith to the native peoples there.

Clearly, what Jefferson was describing was not a rigid barrier between faith and public policy, but denominational allegiance by the state. As the Constitution says, the federal government was not to "establish religion," that is, to select a particular denomination as a national church.

That's all the wall is. And Jefferson was among the most secular of the Founding Fathers, who did not believe in miracles, such as the virgin birth or resurrection of Jesus Christ.

## American Law and Church-State Separation

The wall of separation nowhere appears in American law until the 1947 case *Everson v. Board of Education*, when the Supreme Court considered whether a New Jersey law allowing school districts to arrange daily transportation for children to religious schools was constitutional. Although declaring the wall, the Court went on to say that school boards expending public funds getting students to and from religious schools wasn't unconstitutional—such accommodations were fine.

Later in 1952, the Supreme Court clarified itself in *Zorach v. Clauson*, saying Americans, "are a religious people whose institutions presuppose a Supreme Being. . . . When the state encourages religious instruction or cooperates with religious au-

# The Dogma of Church-State Separation

No metaphor in American letters has had a more profound influence on law and policy than Thomas Jefferson's "wall of separation between church and state." Today, this figure of speech is accepted by many Americans as a pithy description of the constitutionally prescribed church-state arrangement, and it has become the sacred icon of a strict separationist dogma that champions a secular polity in which religious influences are systematically and coercively stripped from public life.

In our own time, the judiciary has embraced this figurative phrase as a virtual rule of constitutional law and as the organizing theme of church-state jurisprudence, even though the metaphor is nowhere to be found in the U.S. Constitution. In *Everson v. Board of Education* (1947), the United States Supreme Court was asked to interpret the First Amendment's prohibition on laws "respecting an establishment of religion." "In the words of Jefferson," the justices famously declared, the First Amendment "was intended to erect 'a wall of separation between church and State' ... [that] must be kept high and impregnable. We could not approve the slightest breach."

The Heritage Foundation,
"The Mythical 'Wall of Separation':
How a Misused Metaphor Changed Church-State Law,
Policy, and Discourse," June 23, 2006.

thorities ... it follows the best of our traditions. For it then respects the religious nature of our people and accommodates the public service to their spiritual needs."

## Modern Interpretation of Separation

But in recent decades, this wall has become a hammer used to bludgeon people of faith in a concerted effort to purge the public square of references to faith, silencing those who express faith in a public setting.

With the resurgent interest in the original meaning of the Constitution that began in the 1980s and continues today, using this "wall" as the basis for applying the First Amendment has increasingly been criticized.

One such example came from Chief Justice William Rehnquist. Writing in dissent in *Wallace v. Jaffree* while still an associate justice, Renhquist wrote, "It is impossible to build sound constitutional doctrine upon a mistaken understanding of constitutional history, but unfortunately the Establishment Clause has been expressly freighted with Jefferson's misleading metaphor for nearly 40 years. Thomas Jefferson was, of course, in France at the time the . . . Bill of rights [was] passed in Congress and ratified by the states. His letter to the Danbury Baptist Association was a short note of courtesy, written 14 years after the Amendments were passed by Congress. He would seem to any detached observer as a less than ideal source of contemporary history as to the meaning of the Religion Clauses of the First Amendment."

America got along just fine without this wall for 158 years, and even afterwards. It's only been in recent years that it has been twisted into a secularizing influence in our society.

These are historical facts. Children should be taught facts in history class.

> "The truth about America's Christian founding is getting out, despite media hostility, politically correct schoolbooks and rising intolerance toward any public expression of faith."

# America Is a Christian Nation

## Robert Knight

*Robert Knight is an author and senior writer for Coral Ridge Ministries. In the following viewpoint, he maintains that America was founded as a Christian nation by men grounded in a Christian understanding of law. Knight argues that the principle of church-state separation has been misinterpreted as signifying that the United States is a secular nation.*

As you read, consider the following questions:

1. Why does the author believe Will Bunch attacked Glenn Beck and David Barton in his August 26, 2010, column?

2. What, according to Knight, did James Madison write in the *Federalist Papers*, No. 51?

3. What does the author believe was the real achievement of the nation's Founding Fathers?

Will Bunch's CNN.com tirade earlier this week ["Glenn Beck Rewrites Civil Rights History," August 26, 2010,] against television host Glenn Beck and David Barton—the founder and president of WallBuilders, a national pro-family organization that emphasizes history's "moral, religious and constitutional heritage"—for allegedly creating "pseudo history" reveals more about Mr. Bunch than it does about what Mr. Beck and Mr. Barton are presenting.

Mr. Bunch seems, above all, to be annoyed that many people are no longer staying on the liberal plantation of secularized American history. He offers little in the way of examples of error, just differences of opinion, such as his own assertion about "the much-debunked idea that America's creation was rooted in Christianity."

## A Secular America?

Much debunked? That would have been news to many of the Founding Fathers, whose biblical understanding of man as created in the image of God informed their insistence in the Declaration of Independence that people have "unalienable rights" to "life, liberty and the pursuit of happiness." This was tempered by the biblically informed idea that man is prone to sin. In the *Federalist Papers*, No. 51, for example, James Madison wrote, "But what is government itself, but the greatest of all reflections on human nature? If men were angels, no government would be necessary."

Therefore, any government formed by men needs checks and balances to avoid tyranny. On a more elementary level, the signers of the Declaration and the Constitution were mostly Christian. You can look it up.

Bunch complains that, "In April, Barton told Beck's 3 million TV viewers that 'we use the Ten Commandments as the basis of civil law and the Western world [and it] has been for 2,000 years.'"

Perhaps this is why the Ten Commandments numerals are represented at the bottom of a door to the U.S. Supreme Court courtroom and why Moses, revered as the lawgiver to Jews in the Hebrew bible, and Christians in the New Testament, appears holding two tablets elsewhere in the Supreme Court building.

He appears between the Chinese philosopher Confucius and Solon, the Athenian statesman—at the center of a frieze of historic lawgivers on the building's East Pediment. Moses is also among an array of lawgiver figures depicted over the Court's chamber.

Tellingly, Mr. Bunch does not dispute the accuracy of the quotes that Mr. Barton cites that spell out a Christian understanding of law and man among some of the Founding Fathers.

## What the Founding Fathers Said

In a letter to Thomas Jefferson, written 37 years after the Declaration of Independence, John Adams wrote: "The general principles, on which the Fathers achieved independence, were the only Principles in which that beautiful Assembly of young gentlemen could Unite. . . . And what were these general Principles? I answer, the general Principles of Christianity, in which all these Sects were United: . . . Now I will avow, that I then believe, and now believe, that those general Principles of Christianity, are as eternal and immutable, as the Existence and Attributes of God; and that those Principles of Liberty, are as unalterable as human Nature and our terrestrial, mundane System."

John Jay, the first chief justice of the Supreme Court, wrote in a letter to a friend, "Providence has given to our people the choice of their rulers, and it is the duty, as well as the privilege and interest of our Christian nation to select and prefer Christians for their rulers."

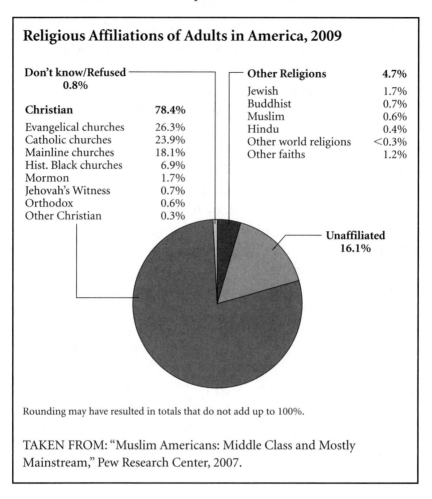

**Religious Affiliations of Adults in America, 2009**

| | |
|---|---|
| Don't know/Refused | 0.8% |
| | |
| **Christian** | **78.4%** |
| Evangelical churches | 26.3% |
| Catholic churches | 23.9% |
| Mainline churches | 18.1% |
| Hist. Black churches | 6.9% |
| Mormon | 1.7% |
| Jehovah's Witness | 0.7% |
| Orthodox | 0.6% |
| Other Christian | 0.3% |

| | |
|---|---|
| **Other Religions** | **4.7%** |
| Jewish | 1.7% |
| Buddhist | 0.7% |
| Muslim | 0.6% |
| Hindu | 0.4% |
| Other world religions | <0.3% |
| Other faiths | 1.2% |

**Unaffiliated** 16.1%

Rounding may have resulted in totals that do not add up to 100%.

TAKEN FROM: "Muslim Americans: Middle Class and Mostly Mainstream," Pew Research Center, 2007.

Mr. Bunch further complains that Barton "gives less than short shrift to the real achievement of the Founders in separating church and state."

I would argue that their real achievement was elsewhere. Their real achievement was far larger: creation of a unique, limited government with protections for the freedoms of religion, speech, press and assembly and protection of property rights, without which no freedom exists. The result was the most prosperous and freest nation in history.

And property rights are endorsed throughout the Bible.

## Silencing Christians in the Public Square

The "wall of separation between church & state," by the way, is not in the Constitution. It's from a letter from President Thomas Jefferson to the Danbury, Connecticut, Baptists, who were concerned that the national government would favor one Christian denomination over others. But Mr. Jefferson's phrase has become a sacred totem used by activist judges to drive Christian symbols from the public square.

The real reason that Mr. Bunch is so exercised is that the truth about America's Christian founding is getting out, despite media hostility, politically correct schoolbooks and rising intolerance toward any public expression of faith—unless it advances leftist goals.

America is a unique beacon of freedom precisely because of its founders' Christian perspective, which has protected the right of conscience and thus freedom of religion for Jews, Muslims, Hindus, Buddhists and nonbelievers. Try to identify another nation on Earth that similarly advanced individual rights without being influenced by Christianity.

Beck and Barton are striking what Abraham Lincoln described in a different context as the "mystic chords of memory." It makes perfect sense that many Americans are tuning in.

> "Those who state outright that Christianity was the driving force behind the settling and political conception of the United States rely on contrived historicism."

# America Is a Secular Nation

**Stuart Whatley**

*Stuart Whatley is a writer and journalist. In the following viewpoint, he contends that there is a real danger in believing that America is a uniquely Christian nation in which principles of individual liberty were formed by Christian culture and religiosity. Whatley argues that although there is a debate as to the Christian roots of the nation's Founding Fathers, it is essential to American ideals of religious freedom that the country is treated as a secular nation to avoid the threat of religious oppression.*

As you read, consider the following questions:

1. According to the author, what percentage of Americans considered themselves Christian in 2008?

2. What percentage of Americans classified themselves as atheists or agnostics in 2008, according to Whately?

3. According to the author, what Roman emperor brought
   Christianity into the political fold?

It may be a sign of the times that on Billy Graham Parkway
in Charlotte, N.C, from whence the famed evangelist hailed,
the North Carolina Secular Society recently unveiled a sugges-
tively secular billboard: a flag with the words "One Nation In-
divisible."

It is also a sign of the times that this message was promptly
doctored by vandals with the words, "UNDER GOD"—a
qualifier that wasn't added to the Pledge of Allegiance until
1954.

With a creeping rise in secularists and nonbelievers today,
some American Christian traditionalists see a politically exis-
tential threat, leading to reactions such as those from a few of
Charlotte's faithful. One is reminded of John Kennedy Toole's
cantankerously amusing character, Ignatius J. Reilly, in *Confed-
eracy of Dunces* [a novel published in 1980]—combative toward modern culture and nostalgic for the halcyon days of
Thomas Aquinas. This traditionalist camp is deeply perturbed
by new threads in the social fabric and insistent that America
is a Christian nation—demographically as well as politically.

This tension transcends a historical argument about the
roots of American liberty. It goes to the heart of some of
today's most trenchant political debates, such as same-sex
marriage, prayers at town meetings, US foreign policy toward
Israel, and end-of-life issues germane to health-care reform.

## Debate over America's Christian Roots

Is America really a Christian nation?

Demographics give a clear answer. In 2008, 76 percent of
Americans called themselves "Christian." That's down 10 percentage points since 1990, but it's still an overwhelming and
defining majority. Meanwhile, just 1.6 percent of Americans
professed to be agnostics or atheists, more than double the
amount in 1990.

History gives a more-muddled answer. The United States' political origin as a "Christian nation" is a far more contentious issue, often reduced to each side drawing lines in the sand with fanciful single-factor readings of complex past events. A prime example comes from Jonah Goldberg, writing in the latest issue of *Reason* [July 2010]: "Our constitutional order rests on the conviction that we are endowed by our creator with certain rights. Both the abolitionist and civil rights movements were religious in nature."

Mr. Goldberg's oblique claim belongs to those who see American freedom as a Christian brand—available for all, but religiously trademarked nonetheless. But those who state outright that Christianity was the driving force behind the settling and political conception of the United States rely on contrived historicism.

## Insidious Implications

There are insidious intellectual implications to maintaining such a position: namely, the view that Christianity itself plays a defining, prerequisite role not just in the character and culture of America, but in its philosophical embrace of individual liberty as well.

A hefty segment of American Christians believes that its specific version of God is the inspiration for all men's conception of freedom. If the United States is a wholly Christian nation then the syllogism follows that the liberty it affords to all is specifically Christian-furnished.

Indeed, the Declaration of Independence does make quick mention of God and a Creator, but not one of its 27 specific grievances has anything to do with religious liberty, and the nature of that "Creator" is hopelessly vague. Most everyone for whom rights were secured at the drafting and signing of the United States Constitution was a Christian, but that document makes no mention of any god. And historically, some of the first settlers to America—Christian separatist pilgrims—

## The Decline of the Christian Nation

While we remain a nation decisively shaped by religious faith, our politics and our culture are, in the main, less influenced by movements and arguments of an explicitly Christian character than they were even five years ago. I think this is a good thing—good for our political culture, which, as the American Founders saw, is complex and charged enough without attempting to compel or coerce religious belief or observance. It is good for Christianity, too, in that many Christians are rediscovering the virtues of a separation of church and state that protects what Roger Williams, who founded Rhode Island as a haven for religious dissenters, called "the garden of the church" from "the wilderness of the world." As crucial as religion has been and is to the life of the nation, America's unifying force has never been a specific faith, but a commitment to freedom—not least freedom of conscience.

*Jon Meacham,* Newsweek, *April 4, 2009.*

were indeed seeking religious liberty, but they arrived at Plymouth 13 years after European bullionist policies had already sent the Virginia Company to settle Jamestown.

So, did Christian culture or religiosity alone derive American notions of liberty? Christianity has long been a mercurial political instrument used to justify the rule of despots and democrats alike, depending on the century.

## Christianity and the State

When the Roman Emperor Constantine first brought Christianity into the political fold, his motivation was purely autocratic. And most of the centuries of Roman Catholic rule that followed were not kind to individual liberty. The 16th-century

Reformation challenged the extant church-state alliance and certainly embraced a fresh platform of human individuality in religious affairs, but to say that Protestantism championed democratic political liberties—as many do—goes too far.

Martin Luther [a German priest and theology professor who initiated the Protestant Reformation in 1517] and his immediate followers opposed all calls for a popular revolution and, according to the English historian Lord Acton, "constantly condemned the democratic literature that arose in the second age of the Reformation." According to Acton, even [French theologian] John Calvin, despite his moderate republican leanings, saw the general populace as "unfit to govern themselves," and instead advocated a form of aristocratic rule.

Thus historical arguments for Christianity's role in securing the modern American notion of freedom are seriously impaired, as there is equally compelling evidence opposed as in support.

Of course, the "Christian nation" argument also asserts that, despite its past shortcomings, it is Christian ecumenism itself that advises individual liberty and equal rights. Indeed, an important facet of Christian belief is free will under God. This seems to align with previous understandings of freedom, which often centered on individual agency.

[Greek philosopher] Aristotle defined it quite simply as, "to live as one wants." Unfortunately, Christianity failed through much of its history to extend this position beyond personal, household religiosity. By contrast, at its outset, the notion of American freedom was predominantly political and populist in nature.

As the 20th-century philosopher John Dewey observed, "the freedom for which our forefathers fought was primarily freedom from a fairly gross and obvious form of oppression, that of arbitrary political power exercised from a distant center."

With this in mind, Dewey points out that American freedom at the time of the Revolution could essentially be boiled down to a libertarian skepticism of government generally, and the right to vote.

## The Threat from Christian Majoritarianism

This formulation was not without complications. Dewey saw freedom as a moving target—"an eternal goal [that] has to be forever struggled for and won anew." Indeed, as [French political thinker Alexis de] Tocqueville realized early on, strict majoritarianism in the absence of effective government to safeguard individual liberties has just as much potential for tyranny as any other form of rule.

Presumably, those in the majority who assert that the United States is a Christian nation prefer it this way. If they already see American freedom as derived from their own faith, then why shouldn't they?

The dangerous implications of thinking in such a way should be obvious. A case in point is this year's Texas school board curriculum revisions, which will recast American history in Christian terms and dangerously undermine accepted science.

Because the Texas board is a parliamentary body subject to majority vote and comprised predominantly of traditionalist Christians, these deliberations fulfilled Dewey and Tocqueville's warnings, as well as an observation from [journalist and satirist] H.L. Mencken, who described American democracy as "a pathetic belief in the collective wisdom of individual ignorance." It can be easily argued that this is a majoritarianism that does not adequately comport with the rights of the religiously neutral minority.

Seeing American freedom as Christian freedom sets the stage for political battles much larger than Texas school books and secular billboards. The historical debate over the Christianity or secularism of the Founders will continue to be caviled over ad infinitum. More urgent and insidious is the claim by members of one side that they have first dibs to the freedom all should equally enjoy.

*"Religion has been wrenched from the personal and prophetic to the partisan and political."*

# Religious Expression in the United States Is Too Public and Political

*Barry Lynn*

*Barry Lynn is an author, talk-show host, and executive director of the Americans United for Separation of Church and State. In the following viewpoint, he maintains that religion in America has been used in a partisan manner and that religious expression often is a requirement for candidates who aspire to political office. Lynn also bemoans the subsidization of religion by the government, noting that there is a danger to both the state and the religion if the government continues to fund religious schools and programs.*

As you read, consider the following questions:

1. According to the author, what did presidential candidate John F. Kennedy assert in 1960?

2. What was the view of the nation's Founding Fathers regarding religious funding, according to Lynn?

Barry Lynn, "Is America Too Damn Religious?," ABCNews.com, February 1, 2007. Copyright © 2007 by ABCNews.com. Reproduced by permission.

3. How many nonbelievers does the author say there are in America today?

As a minister, I certainly don't think people in the United States are too religious.

The United States is a remarkably diverse country where both nonreligion (atheism, humanism and freethinking) and religion have flourished, and people are proud of what they believe.

However, as someone who takes spirituality seriously, I do think that the fact that religion has tastelessly been overpoliticized, oversubsidized and overcommercialized is "damnable" and in my opinion there is certainly too much of that in America.

Let's use Christianity, at the moment the most statistically robust religion in America, as an example. I suspect that Jesus would be astonished by what Americans do in his name.

Many conservative Christians say that even committed gay couples should not have rights equal to heterosexuals because that offends biblical teaching. However, Jesus says in Matthew 22:35, that Christians must love their neighbors as they would have themselves be loved, without any sexual-orientation-specific caveats.

Jesus has become a poster child for anti-choice activists who fail to acknowledge that the topic is never even mentioned in the Christian Bible. By the way, all this does is demonstrate the temptation to cherry-pick Scripture, since the United States is not to be guided by biblical "truth" but constitutional doctrine.

Dec. 25, the day Christians celebrate the birth of Christ, has been overrun with tacky plastic Nativity scenes, "blowout" sales and playthings like Elmo and Wii. In one poll this year more respondents indicated they wanted to see a creche at City Hall than said they actually planned to attend services at Christmas.

That's tacky as well.

Religion has been wrenched from the personal and prophetic to the partisan and political. Once thought too sacred to spoil with politics, religious belief has become a de facto requirement for public office.

No politician dares to end a speech without "God Bless America," lest they be thought irreligious, if not downright demon-possessed. Presidential aspirants now hire religious consultants to show potential voters how devout the candidate is.

There is an affirmative effort to avoid using the words "separation of church and state" lest it be construed as "hostile toward religion."

Have we so quickly forgotten that then-presidential candidate John F. Kennedy told the Southern Baptists in 1960 that he "believe[d] in an America where the separation of church and state is absolute" and promised to step aside from office if ever forced to choose between staying true to his faith or to the United States Constitution?

Government financing of religion now causes, as our founders predicted, significant strife.

Few religious groups, from Catholics to Scientologists, can resist a chance to visit the public trough, and the president's Office of Faith-Based and Community Initiatives has given religious organizations unprecedented access to Uncle Sam's pockets and the American citizens' tax dollars contained within.

As a result Americans have been forced to subsidize religious education, religious indoctrination and even religious discrimination in private schools, prisons, drug rehab centers and marriage counseling sessions.

Our Founding Fathers knew that religion was an intensely personal issue and wanted all religious funding to be strictly voluntary. Ironically, government financing of religion also puts religious groups in jeopardy.

"Ten Commandments Decor," cartoon by Mike Lester, *The Rome News-Tribune*, www.PoliticalCartoons.com. Copyright © 2005 by Mike Lester, *The Rome News-Tribune*, www.PoliticalCartoons.com. All rights reserved.

Everyone knows that government money comes with some strings attached. Once a religious group accepts public funds, it can find that those strings have strangled the very vitality of its programs.

Even if not directly funded, many religious groups seem to affirmatively seek the "blessing" of governments by calling for the construction of icons, emblems, and monuments of faith in public spaces.

Many of our most well-known religious leaders can't help but commingle religion and politics.

Televangelist Pat Robertson has called for the preemptive assassination of Venezuelan President Hugo Chavez and flatly asserted that Ariel Sharon's recent stroke was punishment from God. In an apparently solar-flare induced miscommunication, Robertson also reported in 2006 that God had told him that the Republicans would retain control of Congress in the midterm elections.

Religious Right zealot Jerry Falwell said on Sept. 13, 2001 that the 9/11 terrorist attacks were America's punishment for all the civil libertarians and feminists in the nation, and concluded we "probably got what we deserved."

Men like Robertson and Falwell who believe God's word is absolutely knowable and can infallibly be interpreted by themselves can create real dangers in a democracy. These men have regular meetings with administration and congressional leaders.

There is only small solace in the writings of one administration official who wrote recently that within the walls of [White House deputy chief of staff] Karl Rove's office these folks were routinely referred to as "the nuts."

What America needs is for the 1,500 faiths practiced here and the 20 million nonbelievers who are also first-class citizens to have vigorous debates between themselves about God and moral discourse. What she also needs is for governments to butt out of that deliberation. In that way, the separation of church and state will continue to "bless" America.

> "'The separation of church and state'
> ... has been used as a bludgeon to rid
> politics of all vestiges of religion in gen-
> eral, but Christianity in particular."

# The Separation of Church and State in the United States Has Gone Too Far

*Louis DeBroux*

*Louis DeBroux is a political commentator. In the following view-point, he laments the modern implementation of separation of church and state, arguing that the removal of religion from public life has meant devastating social consequences for American society. DeBroux maintains that the intent of the nation's Founding Fathers was not to completely eliminate religion from the public sphere.*

As you read, consider the following questions:

1. What did the US Supreme Court decide on the issue of the memorial cross erected in a barren stretch of the Mojave Desert, according to DeBroux?

2. Where did the phrase "the separation of church and state" first appear, as reported by the author?

3. What does DeBroux believe are the negative consequences of the removal of religion from the public
sphere?

Like nails on a chalkboard, there are certain phrases that
make my skin crawl and get my ire up. One of those is
"our American democracy" (which we most assuredly are
not). Another is when people claim that any acknowledgment
of religion by government is banned because of the "separation of church and state". This may just be the most misunderstood and misconstrued phrase in American polity. That
phrase has been used as a bludgeon to rid politics of all ves-
tiges of religion in general, but Christianity in particular.

The First Amendment to the U.S. Constitution states in
part "Congress shall make no law respecting an establishment
of religion, or prohibiting the free exercise thereof . . . " That
would seem to be clear and unambiguous language protecting
religious freedom in every facet of life. It doesn't say " . . . unless you are an elected official, or at a football game at a public school, etc."

Yet in the name of "separation of church and state" prayers
at high school football games have been banned. Displays of
the Ten Commandments on public property have been
banned. Catholic Adoption Services in Massachusetts and
Washington, D.C. were forced to shut their doors because they
refused to violate their religious beliefs by placing children in
homes of homosexual couples. The city of San Diego was
sued in order to remove a small cross from the city's official
seal.

Now we have conflicting messages in two recent Supreme
Court decisions. In one, the court ruled that a memorial cross
erected in a barren stretch of the Mojave Desert could stay
(the ACLU had sued to have it removed under the separation
argument), although shortly after the ruling vandals cut it
down and stole it. The other was a non-decision in which the

court refused to review a ruling by the 9th Circuit Court of Appeals in which the Boy Scouts were denied the lease of public lands (a lease they'd already had and were renewing) because the court ruled they are a religious organization due to the Scout's oath to do their "duty to God" and be "morally straight." The suit was brought by two couples; a lesbian couple objecting to the Scouts' ban on homosexual leaders, and an agnostic couple offended by the reference to God.

These rulings were based in large part on the separation argument. Yet that phrase is nowhere to be found in the Constitution. In fact, the phrase came from an obscure letter written by Thomas Jefferson in 1802 to the Danbury Baptist Association of Connecticut. The Baptists feared that the legislature was preparing to make Anglicanism the new national religion, so they wrote Jefferson, the newly elected president, pleading with him to protect their religious liberties and apply his influence against any such attempts.

In response, Jefferson wrote, "Believing with you that religion is a matter which lies solely between man and his God, that he owes account to none other for his faith or his worship, that the legislative powers of government reach actions only, and not opinions, I contemplate with sovereign reverence that act of the whole American people which declared that their legislature would 'make no law respecting an establishment of religion, or prohibiting the free exercise thereof,' thus building a wall of separation between Church and State." The wall was intended to be one way . . . to keep government out of the affairs and administration of religion. It was never intended to ban religious influence from government.

A study of American history shows that the Founding Fathers were heavily influenced by religion. Jefferson, often accused of being an agnostic or atheist, was likely a Deist; but regardless, he was a believer in God and in Jesus Christ. After all, this is the man who penned the Declaration of Independence, who so eloquently opined the concept that all men are "endowed by their Creator with certain unalienable rights." If that were too ambiguous, Jefferson also wrote, "And can the liberties of a nation be thought secure when we have removed their only firm basis, a conviction in the minds of the people that these liberties are of the gift of God? That they are not to be violated but with His wrath? Indeed I tremble for my country when I reflect that God is just; that His justice cannot sleep forever."

Jefferson understood that our liberties come from God, and that if they do not come from God then they are granted by government, and can be taken by government at their pleasure. That philosophy then usurps man of his unalienable rights, and government then grants rights at the whim of the majority, which is nothing more than mob rule.

Our second president, John Adams, rightly noted that "we have no government armed with power capable of contending with human passions unbridled by morality and religion. Our Constitution was made only for a moral and religious people. It is wholly inadequate to the government of any other."

So what has separation of church and state, the removal of religion from the public sphere, wrought? We now live in a nation where prayer and religious displays are largely banned in public settings; where public indecency laws are suspended in California for the Folsom Street Fair, so participants can march through the streets in bondage and fetish gear in various degrees of nudity. Yet there can be no prayer in public schools. The National Endowment for the Arts issues grants to "artists" whose "art" includes pictures of the Virgin Mary smeared with dung, or "Piss Christ", which is a crucifix immersed in urine. Yet high school valedictorians are relieved of that honor if they dare acknowledge Christ in their speech. Strippers and pornography are now protected by free speech laws. Religion is not.

We indulge our basest proclivities; push to see just how vile we can be in language and in culture, all in the name of freedom. And what has this freedom obtained for us? High teen pregnancy rates, abortions, sexual disease, infidelity, divorce, heartbreak. Families broken apart, homes wrecked. This is not freedom. This is spiritual bondage.

"[One] reason for religious support of
the separation of church and state was
to protect the autonomy and independence of the church."

# There Should Be a Separation
# of Church and State to Protect
# Religious Liberty

*Elizabeth Katz*

*Elizabeth Katz is a contributor to the University of Virginia Law
School website. In the following viewpoint, she reports on a lecture by Judge Michael W. McConnell given at the University of
Virginia in 2005, in which he challenges the conventional interpretation of the establishment clause of the First Amendment. In
the lecture, McConnell argues that instead of protecting government from the influence of religion, the establishment clause was
created to protect the autonomy of religion from government interference.*

As you read, consider the following questions:

1. As cited by Katz, which Founding Fathers does McConnell identify as supporting some kind of establishment
   of religion?

2. What are the three reasons McConnell cites that government would want the establishment of religion, as reported by the author?

3. According to McConnell, as cited by Katz, why do republics require public virtue?

The nation's founders included the Establishment Clause of the First Amendment to protect and promote the church's inculcation of public virtue, rather than to protect the federal government from the influence of religion, said Judge Michael W. McConnell at the Oct. 27 Meador Lecture on Law and Religion.

McConnell, who serves on the U.S. Court of Appeals for the 10th Circuit, delivered his speech to an overflowing audience in Caplin Pavilion.

He noted that the separation of church and state often has been a provocative issue in American history. "We seem to be at one of those times again in American public life when these questions of how to adjust the spheres are on many people's minds," he said.

McConnell challenged popular explanations of the separation of church and state.

"The conventional wisdom goes something like this: that the creation of a liberal democratic order requires or at least presupposes the secularization of the civic culture, and that this secularization is embodied in the establishment clause of the First Amendment, the separation of church, which protects the private practice of religion from government but also, it is said, protects government from the device of any irrational powers of religion," he said. "It's necessary according to this view to base public policy and public affairs on the neutral grounds of reason rather than the superstitious sway of priests and bishops or the fulmination of fundamentalists."

"To many . . . religious intrusion into politics is an offense against their cherished ideal of a secular public sphere," Mc-

Connell said. "They speak darkly of betraying the principles of the founding and dismantling the wall of separation created by the founders."

Although McConnell said he believes the issue is overblown on both sides, he thought it was advantageous to rekindle interest in the role of religion in a democratic republic. "The founding was quite different and in many ways more interesting than this conventional wisdom."

Although the First Amendment prohibited the *federal* establishment of religion, he said, approximately half of the founding states had some form of religious establishment when the amendment was ratified and others were exploring the possibility.

"The 1780s were actually a time of renewed interest in and support for state religious establishments," McConnell said.

Founding fathers such as John Adams, George Washington, Patrick Henry, and John Marshall were among those who supported some kind of establishment of religion, according to McConnell.

"We have to understand why intelligent republican Americans would support an establishment in order for us to appreciate what was going on when the American people adopted the opposite view," he said.

McConnell presented a three-step argument in favor of the establishment of religion. First, a republican government "required an extraordinary degree of public virtue." Second, religion was "necessary or at least highly conducive to the formation of public virtue." And finally, government support was necessary or at least valuable in sustaining religion. The modern critique focuses on the first two steps. The first step is flawed, according to many, because a republican government must be neutral about the definition of virtue, and it is impossible to promote virtue without defining it. Critics of the second step focus on the possible disassociation of religion and virtue.

"Pretty clear, isn't it, that religion is not necessary for virtue; we all know people who are virtuous without being religious," McConnell said. "More damaging to the argument is the opposite; we all know people who are conspicuously religious but not virtuous. We may even have seen some of them on TV."

During the 18th century, however, the third step was the most important and controversial. At the time, the relationship between republicanism and public virtue, the first step, was less problematic, partially for semantic reasons. McConnell explained "virtue" comes from a Latin root for "manly," and its 18th-century meaning was rooted in this definition.

"Above all, 'virtue' meant public spiritedness," he said. "We might better use a term like 'voluntary self-sacrifice.'"

Unlike common forms of 18th-century government such as monarchies, republics required public virtue because the republican emphasis on personal freedom made a government based on coercion and punishment distasteful.

Acceptance of the second step—the strong ties between virtue and religion—was rooted in the church's monopoly on disseminating knowledge. With no public schools and no television or radio, churches were the principal and almost only institution promoting public virtue. Because a common theme of biblical religion is condemnation of selfishness, the social values promoted by churches fit well with public virtue as self-sacrifice. Even today, McConnell contended, churches are the most common source of the inculcation of public virtue. Although he believes some studies are flawed, he cited an extensive literature to suggest religious participation correlated with socially responsible behavior.

"I'm not asking you to accept the second step—it's a big thing to swallow—but just understand why the relationship between religion and public virtue may not be so far-fetched even today," he said.

McConnell suggested that from the modern perspective, the third step "is actually the least hard to swallow.

"What do we ever do in our society when we think something is good and we want to encourage it?" he asked. "We spend money on it. . . . Spending money on good things is what our country may do best."

In the 18th century, however, the third step is what ultimately resulted in the decision to disestablish religion. Although federalists such as James Madison and Alexander Hamilton were able to reduce the necessity of relying on public virtue by creating checks and balances, they realized they could not eliminate it. Thus, the first step was accepted by the founders. Similarly, the second step was accepted with relative ease.

"In a largely Christian society, it was virtually inconceivable for most to imagine that virtue could be sustained on any other basis [other than the church]," McConnell said. "It would require the creation of alternative institutions for the inculcation of virtue, and it was hard to imagine what they would be."

Instead, opposition to the establishment of religion was rooted primarily in the third step, and came from an unexpected quarter—the most intensely evangelical elements of American society.

"They offered a religious critique of the establishment of religion," he said.

Because freedom of conscience and a personal relationship with God were primary tenets of the Protestant reformation, established religion was contrary to the ideals of common Christian denominations at the time.

"An establishment of religion is useless because only genuine faith, a voluntary submission to the will of God, is true religion," McConnell said. "So neither the Pope in Rome nor the legislature has any authority to dictate to us in matters of religion."

The religious arguments often were incorporated into secular sources, too. For example, Thomas Jefferson began Virginia's 1786 bill for religious freedom with a theological proposition.

A second reason for religious support of the separation of church and state was to protect the autonomy and independence of the church. Historically, governments are more likely to use churches for their own purposes than for churches to use governments, according to McConnell. For this reason, Baptists took the separation a step further and preferred for churches not to receive money from the state.

"He who pays the piper picks the tune," McConnell said.

Finally, many argued that established religion would be weaker than nonestablished religion.

"This should seem fairly plausible to us today because when the government runs something, it is usually done poorly," McConnell joked. "If you like the United States Postal Service, you probably like an established church also."

Following Adam Smith's economic views, religious leaders believed the exertion, zeal, and energy of ministers would be greater if independent from the state.

"Which members of the clergy have a greater incentive to bring in new members and to get the congregation excited?" McConnell said. "Is it the minister who receives a regular stipend from the state, or is it the minister who depends for a salary on passing the collection plate every Sunday morning?"

McConnell concluded that the separation of church and state was supported to protect the strength of religion more so than that of the government.

"These were the arguments that actually carried the day against establishment of religion, not that religion is deleterious or unnecessary to liberal government but that government support and control are bad for religion," he said.

Although disestablishment looked risky, the founders determined it was in the best interest of religion and consequently of the state.

"Religion would flourish better if it were left free," he said. "Just as free enterprise is good for the economy, free exercise is good for religion. And the remarkable thing about this experiment is it seems to have worked—the United States is still one of the most religious countries in the world."

From this, McConnell said, it is possible to be left with "a happy, optimistic conclusion."

"It wasn't necessary to choose between religion, public virtue and disestablishment—you could have all three," he said.

He concluded his lecture with some caveats.

"I did not say and I do not believe that all religions are good," he said, explaining that the role of religion in American history has been "a mixed bag just like everything else. . . . But I do believe, on balance, that *freedom* of religion has beneficial civil effects, and that's the point."

Furthermore, he does not believe nonreligious philosophies are inferior or do not contribute to the public good.

"My point is just that our constitutional tradition does not favor the secular over the religious, that religion has a public and not just a private role to play, and that nonestablishment was defended as good for religion, hence good for virtue and hence good for liberal democracy," he said.

*"The [Everson] court ruled that the freedom of religious expression in the public square was actually a violation of the separation of church and state."*

# The Post-1947 Concept of Church and State Has Led to Intolerance of Religious Expression

*Christopher Merola*

*Christopher Merola is a conservative Republican political consultant in Washington, D.C. In the following viewpoint, Merola argues that the principle of the separation of church and state has been mischaracterized since 1947, when Justice Hugo Black redefined the meaning of the phrase* separation of church and state. *This redefinition has served to limit religious expression in the public square, which is a violation of the First Amendment (freedom of religion, freedom of speech, etc.). Merola argues that some on the political left have engaged in psycho-politics, which is the practice of changing the accepted meaning of words to fit a*

Christopher Merola, "The Separation of Church and State Debate," Townhall.com, March 12, 2010. Copyright © 2010 by Townhall.com. Reproduced by permission of the author.

*political agenda—in this case, convincing the public that intolerance of religious expression is actually tolerance of all religions or of nonreligion.*

As you read, consider the following questions:

1. According to Merola, why was math teacher Bradley Johnson ordered by his school district to remove two patriotic banners from his classroom in January 2007?

2. What did the federal court rule in Johnson's case, according to the author?

3. According to Merola, how has psycho-politics been used to change the meaning of the phrase *separation of church and state*?

On Thursday, March 11, 2010, the Ninth Circuit Court of Appeals, which is the most liberal court in the history of the United States, upheld as constitutional the phrase, "One Nation Under God," found in the Pledge of Allegiance, as well as the phrase, "In God We Trust" on our currency. The Ninth Circuit rejected two legal challenges by the rabid atheist, Michael Newdow.

Newdow is the same atheist that sued over the Pledge of Allegiance in 2002 and won his case at the Ninth Circuit at that time, only to have the Supreme Court in 2004 tell him he lacked legal standing to file the suit, as he did not have custody of his daughter for whom he was filing the suit.

In this recent case, Newdow was making the claim that the phrase, "One Nation Under God," disrespected his own religious beliefs. Yet, the Ninth Circuit rejected his suit this time. "The Pledge is constitutional," said Judge Carlos Bea, who wrote the majority decision. Bea said, "The Pledge of Allegiance serves to unite our vast nation through the proud recitation of some of the ideals upon which our Republic was founded."

When the Ninth Circuit Court of Appeals, which is the most frequently overturned circuit court in our nation's history, a court that has been overturned by the US Supreme Court several times in one day, actually upholds references to God as constitutional, it gives more credence to the fact that our Constitution is not a living document.

You may recall that in November and December of 2008, I submitted two articles on the topic of the Separation of Church and State to *Townhall* for the purposes of clarifying just what that phrase truly means, and just what the First Amendment of the Constitution of the United States truly states. In spite of the Ninth Circuit's recent ruling, the errors, falsehoods and misinterpretations of the First Amendment still continue.

Take for example the recent case of Poway United School District of San Diego, California. In January of 2007, math teacher Bradley Johnson was ordered by the school district to remove two patriotic banners from the walls of his classroom as the banners mentioned God. The school district claimed that Johnson's banner violated the Establishment Clause of the First Amendment.

Some of the phrases on the banners were actually the same phrases recently upheld by the Ninth Circuit, like "In God We Trust," and "One Nation Under God."

I like how Bradley Johnson's attorney put it: "Mr. Johnson doesn't proselytize to his students. These banners are patriotic expressions. None of them are from any religious text. None of them are from the Bible or the Koran. They're right out of historic significance. That's the reason why he put them up."

Some students claimed that Johnson's banner made them feel uncomfortable. Maybe so, but that does not mean that the banners violated the Establishment Clause found in the First Amendment. The Constitution does not mention a right to not feel uncomfortable. Free speech often is uncomfortable;

but in the name of the First Amendment we must sometimes tolerate what is uncomfortable.

Think about common everyday occurrences where we must endure feeling uncomfortable in the name of free speech. You may feel uncomfortable when you hear your neighbor swear or use colorful language to describe a situation. You may even feel uncomfortable when reading the newspaper and viewing an ad for a racy movie. Nevertheless, as long as we are not forced to engage in behavior we do not approve of, no law has been broken.

In America, liberty requires we tolerate feeling uncomfortable in order to allow the free expression of ideas to abound. This is precisely why Bradley Johnson won his court case after suing the Poway United School District of San Diego, California. Federal District Court Judge Roger T. Benitez ruled on February 26, 2010 that the Poway Unified School District violated Johnson's constitutional rights as found in the First and Fourteenth Amendments of the United States Constitution, as well as Article I of the California Constitution.

According to the Thomas More Law Center, which represented Johnson in court, the school district tried to remove Johnson's banners but had no problem allowing the posting of a 35 to 40 foot string of Tibetan prayer flags with images of Buddha. The school district also had no problem with the posting of a banner of Hindu leader Mahatma Gandhi's "7 Social Sins," or a poster of Muslim leader Malcolm X, along with a poster of Buddhist leader [the] Dalai Lama. The double standard was more than obvious. Banners and posters of other religious leaders were tolerated, while the two banners posted by Bradley Johnson were censored.

Judge Benitez said in his ruling: "That God places prominently in our nation's history does not create an Establishment Clause violation requiring curettage and disinfectant for Johnson's public high school classroom walls. It is a matter of historical fact that our institutions and government actors have in past and present times given place to a supreme God."

Benitez went on to say: "Fostering diversity, however, does not mean bleaching out historical religious expression or mainstream morality. By squelching only Johnson's patriotic and religious classroom banners, while permitting other diverse religious and anti-religious classroom displays, the school district does a disservice to the students of Westview High School and the federal and state constitutions do not permit this one-sided censorship."

One-sided censorship. Judge Benitez hit the nail on the head. The school district had no right to practice selective tolerance for one brand of ideas at the expense of another. Unfortunately, this selective tolerance has become a common occurrence in America today. I know this all too well having faced similar discrimination during my undergraduate and post-graduate studies.

It seems that some of the liberal elite, whether they are in the media or the academic arena, practice a form of "intolerance in the name of tolerance," as I like to call it. By claiming that banners like Johnson's were somehow intolerant, the school district demonstrated intolerance towards Johnson in the name of a selective tolerance towards others. It is a completely upside-down argument.

How can we truly practice tolerance if we single out those with whom we disagree? Tolerance was designed to allow people with whom we do not agree to coexist along side us. However, today's politically correct version of tolerance is not really tolerance at all, as demonstrated by the Bradley Johnson case.

So just how is it that some on the political left get away with practicing intolerance in the name of tolerance? How does the meaning of intolerance get twisted to mean tolerance?

The practice of changing the common semantically under-stood meaning of words as a political tactic goes back to the Communist Party of the USA (CPUSA), which was formed in 1919. Not long after forming, the CPUSA soon began using a political tactic called psycho-politics, where the changing of the meaning of words, over time, can change the perception and the subsequent behavior of some people's reactions to those words.

While it has taken many decades for our nation to get to the point where tolerance for references to God are viewed as intolerance, the San Diego school district where Johnson is employed proves that psycho-politics can be very powerful over time.

Think back to my first two articles on this topic. What we see is a clear case of psycho-politics put into practice when Justice Hugo Black, an FDR [Franklin D. Roosevelt] appointee and member of the Ku Klux Klan, changed the meaning and purpose of the First Amendment of the Constitution.

In *Everson vs. Board of Education* (1947), the Supreme Court took upon itself a presupposed right to redefine the meaning of the First Amendment. Justice Black and the other FDR appointees to the Supreme Court simply hijacked a phrase used by President Thomas Jefferson, "separation of church and state," found in a letter he wrote to the Danbury Baptist Association (1802). The FDR-stacked court ruled that the freedom of religious expression in the public square was actually a violation of the separation of church and state, even though this phrase is not found in the US Constitution.

In true psycho-politics style the freedom of religious expression was reinterpreted as a violation of the First Amendment. This upside down interpretation of Jefferson's phrase, which, once again, does not even appear in the Constitution of the United States, is precisely why Bradley Johnson had to go to court to win back his First Amendment liberties.

Let's not forget, Johnson's banners did not coerce the worship of a deity or religious figure. The banners did not in any way ask the students to pray or read a Bible scripture. The banners simply showed time-held phrases we all see everyday like, "In God We Trust." Yet, this was somehow looked upon by the Poway United School District of San Diego as a violation of the Establishment Clause found in the First Amendment. Meanwhile, religious statements such as Tibetan prayer flags with images of Buddha, a banner of Hindu leader Mahatma Gandhi's "7 Social Sins," a poster of Muslim leader Malcolm X, and a poster of Buddhist leader [the] Dalai Lama were not seen as a violation of the Establishment Clause.

Another example of intolerance in the name of tolerance.

Thomas Jefferson stated in the Declaration of Independence that the American people are " ... endowed by their Creator with certain unalienable Rights ... " That means our rights do not come from government; they come from God and cannot be changed. If our rights came from government, then the government could easily take them away. You know, that just might be the end game of those who practice intolerance in the name of tolerance.

# Periodical and Internet Sources Bibliography

*The following articles have been selected to supplement the diverse views presented in this chapter.*

| | |
|---|---|
| Henry Bornstein | "Some Historical Perspective on 'Church and State,'" *Vail (CO) Daily*, September 13, 2010. |
| Daniel L. Dreisbach | "Origins and Dangers of the 'Wall of Separation' Between Church and State," OrthodoxyToday, August 28, 2007. www.orthodoxytoday.org. |
| Mansfield Frazier | "Tearing Down the Wall Between Church and State," *Cleveland Leader*, May 26, 2010. |
| John R. Guardiano | "O'Donnell Right About 'Separation of Church and State,'" *American Spectator*, October 19, 2010. |
| Ellen Makkai | "What the Constitution Says About Church and State," *Denver Post*, October 31, 2010. |
| Jon Meacham | "Religious Case for Church-State Separation," *Newsweek*, April 23, 2010. |
| Chuck Norris | "Thanksgiving: A Violation of Church and State?," *WorldNetDaily*, November 24, 2008. |
| Julie A. Oseid | "The Power of Metaphor: Thomas Jefferson's 'Wall of Separation' Between Church & State," *JALWD*, Fall 2010. |
| Gerald Russello | "Tear Down That Wall," *National Catholic Register*, June 5, 2007. |
| Bob Unruh | "Jefferson Advocated 'Gate' Between Church and State," *WorldNetDaily*, February 21, 2007. |
| Brent Walker | "Myths of Separation of Church and State," *Religious Herald*, November 16, 2010. |

OPPOSING
VIEWPOINTS®
SERIES

CHAPTER 2

# How Does the Wall Between Church and State Affect Political Issues?

# Chapter Preface

On April 23, 2010, Arizona governor Jan Brewer signed Arizona SB 1070, also known as the Support Our Law Enforcement and Safe Neighborhoods Act, into law. The new legislation made it a state misdemeanor for undocumented immigrants to be in Arizona without having registration documents, which they receive when they register with the US government upon entering the country. SB 1070 also requires the Arizona police—state and local—to check a suspect's documents to determine his or her immigration status during the course of any kind of stop if officers suspect the person may be an illegal alien. Those without the required documents can be arrested and deported.

Brewer and other supporters praised the law for taking a hard stand against illegal immigration, which they believe to be a real threat to the economic and political health of the state. Brewer blamed the federal government for failing to act on illegal immigration, especially the issue of strengthening America's border with Mexico. Supporters of the law viewed it as a much-needed tool in the fight against illegal immigration.

Critics of the law, however, were outraged by the legislation. Latinos and other groups were alarmed that the law was mandating racial profiling because it requires law enforcement to determine a person's immigration status if officers have any reason to believe an individual might be in the country illegally. Latino activists, politicians, and community leaders argued that they were being singled out and racially profiled by law enforcement. Further, any legal Arizona resident can sue the police and other agencies if he or she believes immigration checks are not being fully enforced. The new law also makes it a crime for anyone to transport an illegal alien or "conceal, harbor or shield" an alien from the proper authorities.

Some of the most vociferous critics of the law are Christian leaders, who view it as immoral and a violation of Christian ethics and values. Such critics argue that the biblical injunction to "welcome the stranger" compels Christians to include migrants and strangers into the community and to aid them in economic, social, political, and spiritual ways. Leaders of other religions expressed similar sentiments about the law, drawing from their own religious tenets. This diverse group of religious leaders organized rallies, wrote to their local newspapers, spoke to the media, lobbied politicians in Washington, D.C., and joined boycotts of the state and companies in the state to express their opposition.

Supporters of the law attacked these religious leaders for their activism, arguing that they had violated the separation of church and state. They pointed out that illegal immigration is just that—illegal—and therefore religious leaders were exhorting believers to support criminals who had violated American law. Believers were put in a difficult position: follow religious teachings instead of secular law. Supporters of the Arizona law argued that religious leaders had no right to place religion above American regulations.

A week after Arizona SB 1070 was passed, the Arizona legislature passed House Bill 2162, which modified the original law. The amended text states that "prosecutors would not investigate complaints based on race, color or national origin." Moreover, it was revised to state that police may only investigate immigration status incident to a "lawful stop, detention, or arrest." The revision was meant to quell concerns about racial profiling. It did not, however, soften the opposition to the law, especially among religious leaders who remain active on the issue of immigration.

The question of whether religious leaders should become active in politics is one of the topics covered in the following chapter, which examines how the wall between church and state affects political issues. Other issues covered in the chapter include religious litmus tests for politicians, the role of religion in policy decisions, and the wisdom of political leaders' talking about their religious beliefs in public.

> *"In addition to being a problem for the Church, when a priest gets too involved in politics, he can also offend the government."*

# Religious Leaders Should Not Get Involved in Politics

### Ronald J. Rychlak

*Ronald J. Rychlak is an author and the associate dean and MDLA Professor of Law at the University of Mississippi School of Law. In the following viewpoint, he outlines the problems that occur when religious leaders get involved in political elections, maintaining that such involvement is self-indulgent and dangerous. Rychlak argues that it is not the role of religious leaders to talk about politics from the pulpit.*

As you read, consider the following questions:

1. What did Father Michael Pfleger discuss in his 2008 sermon in then-presidential candidate Barack Obama's church, according to Rychlak?

2. According to the author, why is Father Pfleger controversial?

3. What are the consequences from the federal government if a religious leader gets involved in politics, in Rychlak's opinion?

None of this year's [2008] Catholic presidential candidates (Sam Brownback, George Pataki, Rudolph Giuliani, Joe Biden, Wesley Clark, Christopher Dodd, Dennis Kucinich, and Bill Richardson) earned a nomination from either of the two major political parties. Arguably, however, the Church had its highest profile in a presidential race since 1960 with this past Democratic primary. Unfortunately, the Church did not come off looking that good.

## The Showmanship of Father Pfleger

Sen. Barack Obama took a lot of criticism over the anti-American, racist tirades of his pastor, the Reverend Jeremiah Wright. He seemed, however, determined to weather the storm until Rev. Michael Pfleger, a white Catholic priest from Chicago's South Side, gave a guest sermon in Obama's Church in which he mocked a "crying" Hillary Clinton and made race-based arguments against her candidacy. Obama was forced to leave his church, and he barely limped to the nomination.

This was the first time that most Catholics saw Father Pfleger in action. The flamboyant priest has, however, been a fixture at St. Sabina's parish since I lived in Chicago in the mid-1980s. His Masses feature rock bands, liturgical dances, almost constant music, but not necessarily any profession of the faith. His synthesis of music, showmanship, and social commentary has created a strong following, but it is one based on his personality, not on Catholic teaching. In fact, Father Pfleger may be more important as a political leader than as a religious one.

The Archdiocese of Chicago, like most dioceses, typically limits priests to a maximum of 12 years at any one parish. Father Pfleger, however, has been at his church for over 25 years. When his bishop tried to move him, Father Pfleger refused to go.

According to a recent article by Matthew Rarey in the *Catholic World Report* [CWR], the Archdiocese of Chicago has not forced Father Pfleger's hand in part due his threat to quit and lead his flock away from the Catholic Church, but also—at least in part—because he is a significant player in Chicago and Illinois politics. Father Pfleger routinely talks about politics from the pulpit. He also seems to deliver lots of votes for Democratic candidates. Once they are in office, they reciprocate by sending money to important Catholic social programs.

After his performance at Senator Obama's former church, Francis Cardinal George told Father Pfleger to take a couple weeks of extra vacation to think about what he had done. He has returned now, and according to the *CWR* article, he's unapologetically picking up right where he left off. That's problematic from the Church's perspective and from the government's perspective.

## The Problem with Politics

When a priest embraces a political viewpoint, it can alienate members of the congregation. The Catholic Church does not claim to have the correct political or economic solution to each problem; it speaks to eternal principles. When a priest claims to know the correct political solution to a typical social problem, he is likely going beyond the Church's teachings and potentially creating problems for the Church. (Is his judgment correct? Does he know better than the Church?) What happens to the soul of a potential convert who leaves Mass, never to return, because he was offended by the unsanctioned teachings that he heard?

There can be confusion when a moral issue is also a political matter. Thus, social activists sometimes try to keep priests from speaking out against abortion, euthanasia, fetal

## Maintaining Tax-Exempt Status

In order to maintain tax-exempt status, churches, like other 501(c)(3) charitable organizations, must forego certain activities. Specifically, 501(c) (3) organizations are prohibited from engaging in excessive political lobbying and any political campaigning. According to the IRS [Internal Revenue Service], Sec. 501(c) of the IRS Code requires that a tax-exempt religious organization "may not attempt to influence legislation as a substantial part of its activities and it may not participate at all in campaign activity for or against political candidates."

*John Ferguson, "Tax Exemptions,"*
*First Amendment Center, August 2008.*

stem cell research, and similar issues because they are political in nature. The Nazis also used to argue that Church teachings and sermons against racial policies were inappropriate ventures into politics. These political issues, however, are also moral issues for the Church. The line can be hard to draw in some cases, but Father Pfleger's liberation theology is clearly beyond the scope of the Church's Magisterium [teaching body].

## Government Rules

In addition to being a problem for the Church, when a priest gets too involved in politics, he can also offend the government. Like most charities, churches are tax-exempt, and donations made to them may be deducted from the donor's income taxes. Donations to political causes, on the other hand, are not deductible. If a church ventures too far into politics, it can lose its tax status. Churches can engage in educational efforts—even "get out the vote" drives—but they are not supposed to advance particular candidates or parties. When they do, the government may respond.

Father Pfleger's brand of Catholicism has shifted the balance of power between the bishop and the priest. It has likely driven some people from the Faith (possibly for reasons completely unrelated to the teachings of the Catholic Church). It could (and probably should) also jeopardize the tax status of his parish. Worst of all, those who attend services conducted by Father Pfleger may think that they are experiencing the full expression of the Catholic Faith, but they are not. They're witnessing Father Pfleger's self-indulgent liturgical abuses and listening to his personal theology. That's the real shame.

"Many were the fiery speeches delivered
from pulpits in support of American
Independence."

# Religious Leaders
# Have the Right to Get
# Involved in Politics

*Lisa Fabrizio*

*Lisa Fabrizio is a political columnist. In the following viewpoint,
she asserts that restrictions placed on religious leaders expressing
political opinions from the pulpit are vindictive retribution by
antireligious political leaders and a violation of free speech. Fabrizio argues that these continuing assaults on religious freedom
are having a destructive effect on colleges and universities, religious institutions, and private citizens.*

As you read, consider the following questions:

1. According to the author, why was the Diocese of Bridgeport, Connecticut, under federal investigation in 2009?

2. How does the state of Connecticut define lobbying, according to Fabrizio?

Lisa Fabrizio, "The Hits Just Keep Coming," *American Spectator*, June 3, 2009. Spectator
.org. Copyright © 2009 by *American Spectator*. Reproduced by permission.

3. What charge does the author believe antireligious people will use against the Catholic Church to try to silence it?

Having returned to these fair shores after an overseas trip, the end of which culminated in a total of 13 hours of flight time, it was with a general sense of relief and peace that I betook myself a seat in my favorite pew in my local parish for Mass last Sunday. But, as has too often happened in the past few months, examples of our Lord's predictions of persecution and calumny against those who believe in him came true once again as our learned pastor took to the pulpit to address us.

## The Investigation

It seems that our Diocese of Bridgeport [Connecticut]—which in March [2009] was forced to marshal the faithful to defend itself from unconstitutional government interference—was notified by the Connecticut Office of State Ethics that it is under investigation for possible violations of the state's lobbying laws. This of course is nothing less than the vindictive retribution by an entity whose leadership has become as anti-religious a nest of vipers as our Lord ever encountered. But our courageous bishop, William E. Lori, is not taking this lying down and has filed an injunction in Federal Court to end this harassment. In a letter to the faithful, he laid out the facts:

> Following the surprise introduction of Bill 1098, a proposal that singled out Catholic parishes and would have forced them to reorganize contrary to Church law and the First Amendment, our Diocese responded in the most natural, spontaneous, and frankly, American, of ways: we alerted our membership—in person and through our website; we encouraged them to exercise their free speech by contacting their elected representatives; and, we organized a rally at the State Capitol. How can this possibly be called lobbying?

He then delivered the kind of rebuke that should warm the hearts of freedom-lovers everywhere:

This cannot possibly be what our Legislature had in mind when it sought to bring more transparency and oversight to a legislative process that has been corrupted by special interests and backroom deals. If it is, then it should shock the conscience of all citizens of the Constitution State.

The State of Connecticut, like so many other American governmental bodies that deliberately obscure their statutes with lawyerly twaddle, basically defines lobbying as those who spend over $2,000 in any year to: "communicate directly or solicit others to communicate with any official or his staff in the legislative or executive branch of government or in a quasi-public agency, for the purpose of influencing any legislative or administrative action. . . ." There are of course exceptions; one of which is unsurprisingly granted to members of the media.

So in other words, if you, dear taxpayer, were to have the audacity to be offended at the next usurpation of your constitutionally guaranteed liberties by your betters in government, and decided to organize your fellow ungrateful citizens into a letter-writing campaign, and if the cost of this exceeded two grand, you too might be the subject of government retribution. Welcome to the Constitution State!

## The War on Religious Freedom

The point of all this is that in the continuing war between church and state, governments—which in the words of our Declaration of Independence are sending "swarms of Officers to harass our people, and eat out their substance"—are counting on the servile acquiescence of the governed to severely curb our religious freedom. And sadly, it is working.

Colleges and universities, once the bastions of independent thinking and free speech, are now the home to the most stifling rules and regulations punishing the exercise of same.

Private citizens too have been muzzled both socially: bowing to politically correct admonitions never to discuss religion or politics in public, and governmentally: by the soon to be enacted "hate crime" legislation.

# Religious Pluralism Needed

All too often, it seems that when religion steps out in public, division and strife ensue. I believe, however, that the solution to the problem of divisive religious voices in public life is not fewer religious voices—or none at all. The answer is greater participation of diverse religious voices, guided by the principles of religious pluralism.

Religious pluralism allows democratic scrutiny of religious voices, while encouraging their expression, toward the goal of a common vibrant society. The principles of religious pluralism call for:

- Respecting and celebrating diverse religious traditions

- Valuing religious particularity

- Encouraging positive relationships among religious communities

- Engaging in collaborative efforts for the common good. Just as there is a compelling national interest in shaping healthy interaction among different races and ethnicities, so is there a compelling national interest in shaping how different faith communities (including people of no faith) engage one another. All of this requires a public language of faith that is inclusive, respectful and encourages participation— and that is heard at every level of society, including national politics.

*Eboo Patel, in* Debating the Divine:
Religion in 21st Century American Democracy, *2008.*

Of course, those who hate religion in general and the Catholic Church in particular will attempt to howl her into submission by endlessly reviving the so-called "pedophile priest" issue; as if the sins of a few should render the whole body illegitimate. Were this rule similarly applied to the rest of our society, the halls of Congress themselves would also fall silent. Not a bad thought, actually.

## Reviewing History

Yet, in view of the continuing assaults on our religious freedom, one has to doubt if this country could have been founded at all in light of today's standards. Many were the fiery speeches delivered from pulpits in support of American Independence, based on the natural law. One also wonders if clergymen like the Rev. Martin Luther King and others who organized marches in favor of civil rights would today be considered lobbyists. Or what, if any, action should be taken against the many black churches that actively welcome politics and politicians to their lecterns; the Rev. Jeremiah Wright and friends here come to mind.

## The Consequences of War

To take this to the next level, how long will it be before we will see rabbis and pastors across the land become fearful of exercising not only their religious freedom, but their sacred right of free speech as Americans to express their opposition or support for pending legislation. This is already under way in Canada and will probably, like government healthcare, soon speed southward.

We who love the disappearing U.S. Constitution do so in part because—unlike the Declaration, which uses lofty language addressed to the whole world—its meanings are clearly spelled out in words that did and still should speak to American hearts and minds. Words like these that should continue to inspire all future American "lobbyists":

> Congress shall make no law respecting an establishment of religion, or prohibiting the free exercise thereof; or abridg-

ing the freedom of speech, or of the press; or the right of the people peaceably to assemble, and to petition the Government for a redress of grievances.

"It's taking [the First Amendment] to an entirely new level to say that it precludes public officeholders from allowing their Christian worldview to influence their policy."

# Politicians Should Be Allowed to Let Their Religious Beliefs Influence Policy Decisions

## David Limbaugh

*David Limbaugh is an author and political analyst. In the following viewpoint, he maintains that all political leaders draw on their own personal morality and value systems to enact policy; therefore, to expect them to not have their religious views influence their actions is unrealistic. Limbaugh asserts that if voters do not agree with the religious beliefs of a certain candidate, they can vote against them.*

As you read, consider the following questions:

1. According to the author, why should public officials clearly state their values?

2. Why does Limbaugh believe that the popular phrase "we cannot legislate morality" often is misunderstood?

3. What does the author state he would do if a Hindu, Buddhist, or Muslim politician were passing laws based on certain values he did not agree with?

The surfacing of the "religion question" in the [2008] Republican presidential primary campaigns of both Mitt Romney and Mike Huckabee has raised important issues and exposed much public confusion about the intersection of religion and politics.

Secularists feign sympathy with Romney for having to address the Mormon question in response to alleged anti-Mormon bigots but condemn him for failing in his speech to expressly include nonbelievers among those whose religious liberty he would safeguard.

This particular attack on Romney by the secularist bigot patrol reveals their own religious bigotry, their ignorance or their disingenuousness. It goes without saying that robust religious liberty includes the freedom to believe in any religion or not to believe at all.

## Attacks on Christian Leaders

But the secularists' attacks on Huckabee are more serious. They have taken him to task for identifying himself as a "Christian leader" in Iowa, with some saying he was exploiting Romney's Mormonism and also violating the spirit of the constitutional prohibition on requiring religious tests for public office.

In a campaign ad, Huckabee says, "Faith doesn't just influence me. It really defines me," and he identifies himself as a "Christian leader."

It's one thing to read the First Amendment Establishment Clause as prohibiting the slightest government endorsement of the Christian religion (while not demonstrating similar angst over government promotion of secular humanism, New Ageism, Islam or Native American spirituality). But it's taking it to an entirely new level to say that it precludes public office-holders from allowing their Christian worldview to influence their policy preferences or governance.

## Values Influence Policy

Public officials cannot separate their worldview from their governance without gutting themselves into ciphers. Their policy agenda will necessarily reflect their value system. Voters in turn properly base their decisions on candidates in part on their respective values and how closely they resemble their own.

A friend of mine objects that it's wrong for Christians to impose their values through the laws. He cites Justice David Souter's opinion saying the government can't prefer one religion over another.

My friend is merely restating the popular misunderstanding that we cannot legislate morality. All laws are based on morality; the only question is whose morality is being imposed. The pro-abortionist seeks to impose his values by law just as much as the anti-abortionist.

When a Christian legislator votes to restrict abortion, he is not using government to endorse his religion any more than a secularist legislator is endorsing atheism by opposing those restrictions. The Christian legislator is not establishing Christianity but rather certain laws grounded in Christian values—as well as those of other religions.

## Let Voters Decide

Our elected public officials can support or oppose laws for whatever reasons they want, provided they don't otherwise violate the Constitution. If they pass unpopular laws, the electorate may vote them out. But to make a constitutional challenge based on their motives for supporting or opposing laws is a scary prospect. I wouldn't like it if a Hindu, Buddhist or Muslim were passing laws based on certain values with which

## Mitt Romney on Faith and Politics

Almost 50 years ago another candidate from Massachusetts [John F. Kennedy] explained that he was an American running for President, not a Catholic running for President. Like him, I am an American running for President. I do not define my candidacy by my religion. A person should not be elected because of his faith nor should he be rejected because of his faith.

Let me assure you that no authorities of my church, or of any other church for that matter, will ever exert influence on presidential decisions. Their authority is theirs, within the province of church affairs, and it ends where the affairs of the nation begin.

*Mitt Romney,*
New York Times, *December 6, 2007.*

I disagreed. But I would have no constitutional complaint if their final product—the laws they passed—were constitutional. My remedy would be to work against their reelection.

So, for Mike Huckabee to advertise his Christian credentials is not only proper but also admirable and quite useful because it helps voters to identify who he is and what he might do if elected.

How can Huckabee define himself while omitting perhaps his most defining attribute: his Christianity? He is saying, for example, "You can count on me not to waver on the abortion issue because my faith compels me to be pro-life."

It's also unfair to say he is appealing to anti-Mormon bigotry to promote himself as a Christian leader. He is just putting his best foot forward with Christian conservatives whose votes he is seeking. Couldn't we just as easily argue that it bespeaks an anti-Christian bigotry to suggest that merely by promoting his Christian pedigree, Huckabee is attacking other religions or non-religions?

## The "Religion Card"

You can be sure that if Huckabee gets the nomination, his opponents will "play the religion card" against him, like they have against President [George W.] Bush for the last seven years, as in dubbing him a "messianic militarist."

Finally, Huckabee is not implicitly violating the Constitution's bar on imposing a religious test for public office by identifying himself as a Christian leader. The Constitution only forbids us from adopting by law a religious requirement for office. It doesn't bar candidates from promoting their religious backgrounds or forbid voters from considering those backgrounds.

Huckabee is perfectly within his rights to hold himself out as a Christian. Voters are perfectly within their rights to evaluate what that means.

I just hope that fellow Christian conservatives will look beyond the label and not blindly support a Christian candidate who might be way more Christian than conservative. We shouldn't have to choose between the two.

> "We must oppose the introduction of re-
> ligious beliefs into the running of gov-
> ernment and public schools."

# The Introduction of Religious Beliefs into Policy Decisions Must Be Opposed

## Jeffrey S. Victor

*Jeffrey S. Victor is a sociologist and contributing writer to* Online Journal. *In the following viewpoint, he compares the treatment of religion in politics in America with how religion and
politics are treated in France, a country that does not allow stri-
dent or extreme expressions of religious belief. Victor concludes
that Americans must be much more vigilant about the injection
of religion into politics and policy decisions, arguing that it is
not intolerant to oppose religious extremism.*

As you read, consider the following questions:

1. Why does the author believe that America is the most
   traditionally religious of all industrial societies?

2. According to Victor, how many Muslim citizens are
   there in the European Union?

3. What percentage of French citizens are secularist, according to the author?

The meaning of religious tolerance presents a particular dilemma for liberals, because we feel called upon to preach tolerance as a central ideal in our worldview. What constitutes religious tolerance towards Christian extremists at home and Islamic extremists abroad? How should we deal with religious extremists who preach hatred and violence toward people of religions other than their own? Are we intolerant when we strongly oppose religious ideologues who use government to promote their particular brand of religious belief?

We need to keep in mind that the rules for religious tolerance arose out of centuries-long struggles to regulate religious conflict in society. The rules for tolerance differ in different societies, because they are a product of different struggles to attain religious tolerance. In every democratic society, the rules for religious tolerance exist on two levels: the official ones in law and informal ones in social custom. In democratic societies, peaceful political struggle between religious groups is normal and consistent with rules for religious tolerance.

## The Roots of Religious Extremism

Today, the social forces provoking religious extremism are modernization and globalization. The prime mover of modernization is science, as a way of thinking and relating to the world. It emphasizes doubt and questioning rather than faith, rationalism rather than tradition, and inductive logic rather than deductive claims of truths from scriptures. It focuses attention on the material, natural world, rather than the invisible supernatural. Globalization brings us influences from distant and unfamiliar cultures and religions. It results in increasing religious pluralism and multiculturalism within societies.

Extremist Christians, Moslems, Jews and Hindus have many similar ways of thinking. They want to purify religion from the influences of modernization and globalization. They regard themselves as being victims, oppressed by anti-religious forces in society. That is why they are so angry. They condemn their society as morally corrupt. They preach an absolutist religious morality and belief system. They insist on the one right way for everyone. They emphasize punishment for sin, rather than compassion. Therefore, they condemn religious pluralism and religious tolerance.

Religious extremists are not all of one mind. There is a wide spectrum of differences among them. Most religious extremists are non-violent and simply try to isolate themselves from the surrounding "corrupt" society. Some organize themselves to impose their ideology on society through the political system. Only a small minority preach violence as a means to gain their ends.

## Tolerance: America and France Compared

In American society, the First Amendment of the Constitution holds that the government should not support or encourage any particular religion. In addition, the government should not restrict any religious practice. Americans, unlike people in some other democracies, believe that there should be no restrictions on proselytism [to convert or attempt to convert someone to one's religion], even if some people feel harassed by it. Different religious groups may compete with each other for members, as long as they don't use violence. In practice, religious hate speech is regarded as being disreputable, but it is protected by freedom of expression.

American society is the most traditionally religious of all industrial societies. One reason is that in American culture, the practice of religion, any religion, is socially encouraged as an expression of "good" citizenship. American nationalism and generic religion are merged. As a result, atheism and agnosticism are regarded as disreputable and informally discouraged as potentially immoral.

In American society, Christian extremists regard themselves as an oppressed minority threatened by anti-religious influences in society. In contrast, religious modernists regard these fellow citizens as unfairly trying to use the government to proselytize and to impose their morality on society. The basic issue being contested involves a strict versus a weak separation of religion and government. Hot button issues are familiar: teaching about evolution, acceptance of homosexuals, the right to abortion, medically assisted suicide, stem cell research, government support for birth control education, prayer in public schools, and sex in the mass media.

## A Comparison of Cultures

We can gain a deeper understanding into different meanings of religious tolerance from cross-cultural comparisons. In Western Europe, the potential for religious conflict is much greater than it is in the United States. Western Europe is where the social influences of secularization and de-Christianization clash with Moslem immigration and Islamic fundamentalism. In the countries of the European Union, there are 23 million Moslem citizens. Islamic extremists have carried out terrorist murders in Spain, the United Kingdom and the Netherlands.

The rules for religious tolerance in French society offer liberals an interesting and useful contrast with those familiar to Americans. Unfortunately, the religious context of France is commonly misunderstood by Americans. The dominant ethos of contemporary French culture is secular and hostile to religious influences in politics. Religion is limited to the private sphere of life and discouraged in public life. According to surveys, the overwhelming majority of French people are atheists (33 percent), agnostics (14 percent) or simply indifferent, non-practitioners of organized religion (26 percent). This means that the dominant majority of French people (73 percent) are very secular in orientation. (However, many non-practitioners get baptized, married in a church and buried by

## Faith and Politics

Now, religious people, faithful people, are involved in government and involved in politics, and this has been true for a very long time. It has been true since Joseph advised Pharaoh or Moses confronted Pharaoh. Religious people in our country, on the left and the right—witness the civil rights movement or campaigns against the death penalty—religious people have believed that it is their responsibility to engage in politics. I am one of them.

But there is a difference between engaging in politics and transforming politics and government into an extension or an enforcer of your religious point of view. We have recognized in this country, right from our inception, that the connection of politics and religion, government and religion, is inherently a divisive combination. That is why in the Constitution we provide for the fact that everybody is free to exercise religion but the state is not going to establish religion.

What has happened now in American politics, because both parties are appealing to their base at the expense of the center of American politics, is that religion has become a wedge. It has become something to energize the base, but in energizing the base it is then a divisive force in American politics and it has tended to be destructive of the center.

*John Danforth,*
*"Faith and Politics,"*
*September 20, 2006.*

the rites of the Catholic or Protestant church.) In France, at least 8 percent of people are Moslems and a similar percentage, only 8 percent, are actively practicing Catholics.

# A Neutral Public Sphere

As in the United States, the French constitution guarantees the free practice of religion. There exists a very strict separation of religion and government. However, unlike in the United States the government is committed to the principle of a totally religiously neutral (secular) public sphere of life. As one example of this principle, the French government recently outlawed the wearing of any conspicuous religious symbols in public schools, including large crosses for Christians, scull caps for Jewish boys and head scarves or veils for Moslem girls. (This was widely misunderstood in the United States as an act of religious intolerance.) Another example is that religious groups are legally prohibited from engaging in any political activities. If they do so, they will lose their tax-exempt status. Tax-exempt religious groups are restricted to engaging in purely religious ritual activities. A further example is that religious hate speech is a crime if it leads to violence.

In terms of informal norms, politicians are expected to avoid any public religious expression. Most French people don't care about the private religious beliefs of their president or prime minister. Active proselytism is informally discouraged, as intrusions upon personal privacy. Religious proselytizers must register with the local authorities and, just like any salesmen, they may not receive permission to go door-to-door.

# Preserving Tolerance

So, what does religious tolerance mean in these times of growing religious extremism? First, we need not tolerate any claim or behavior justified by a religion. Liberals should not hesitate to criticize and oppose Islamic and Christian extremist demands. We must oppose the introduction of religious beliefs into the running of government and public schools. We should organize opposition to religious hate speech in public. We must recognize that the people who bomb abortion clinics and the people who make themselves into suicide bombers have the same religious mindset.

*"Ideas really do have consequences, and belief impacts behavior. Therefore, the discussion of religion in public life is not only appropriate, but necessary."*

# Political Candidates Should Be Free to Talk About Religious Beliefs

## Ken Connor

*Ken Connor is chairman of the Center for a Just Society in Washington, D.C., and was formerly president of the Family Research Council, chairman of the Board of CareNet, and vice chairman of Americans United for Life. In the following viewpoint, Connor discusses several criteria that are important for evaluating a presidential candidate. One of these criteria is the role of religion in the candidate's life. Connor argues that a candidate's religious beliefs are not irrelevant to the office of president and may provide strength of character during the difficult days of the presidency.*

As you read, consider the following questions:

1. According to the author, who should put the common good above the good of a particular interest group?

Ken Connor, "2008 Comes Early: Criteria to Consider," *Human Events*, January 22, 2007.

2. Acording to Connor, what virtues should a candidate for president possess?

3. Acording to the author, why must the ideas about religion and the religious beliefs of candidates be a necessary part of the public scrutiny of the candidates?

It has been called the perpetual campaign. Even before the new [2007] Congress was sworn in, the nation's attention had shifted to the 2008 presidential elections. Every bill that the Democrats bring to the floor is discussed in terms of 2008. Strategists from both parties are already working overtime to either continue their momentum or regain lost ground.

Every eligible American has a responsibility to vote and an obligation to make an informed choice about which candidate to support. Few decisions are more important than deciding who will lead the country. Therefore, as men and women start throwing their hats into the ring for president, it is time to consider the criteria against which we can measure whether or not a candidate deserves our support. Here are five important points worth considering:

*1. Substance Versus Style.* In today's age of television and internet video, candidates often worry more about style than substance. All too often, time and money are spent developing a candidate's wardrobe or hairstyle while substantive policy proposals languish. This trend is especially obvious when watching party conventions (which are little more than Hollywood extravaganzas), or presidential debates (which are little more than a collection of "soundbites"), or political commercials (which often involve little more than character assassination). The emphasis on image often comes at the expense of thoughtful and sober democratic debate. The American public should step up and demand substance over style. Hard questions should be asked about a candidate's position on substantive issues, and the public should insist on clear, incisive answers rather than vague generalities. Voters must commit to holding candidates to a higher standard when it comes to substantial policy positions.

*2. Promoting for the Common Good.* The preamble to the U.S. Constitution declares that the charter's purpose is to promote " . . . the general welfare, and secure the blessings of liberty to ourselves and our posterity." These themes are often ignored by candidates who try to buy constituencies with promises beneficial only to them, and without regard to the cost to future generations. How refreshing it would be if, when asked by a particular interest group, "What are you going to do for us?" the candidate responded, "Nothing. The greater good of the country requires something else." People should be voting for the common good, not just for that which meets their individual needs. Sometimes in life we need to sacrifice our own desires for the sake of others so that the community will flourish. We desperately need leaders who will put the public interest ahead of that of the special interests.

*3. Voting for Virtues.* We should also keep a candidate's personal virtues in mind when voting for a president. The outcome of the last congressional election demonstrates that "virtue" is not a four-lettered word. Presidents wield great power, and before entrusting a man or woman with that power, we should be sure that they are honorable, just, courageous, humble, thrifty, prudent and wise. The virtues that candidates have cultivated in their private lives will often determine how they govern in their public lives. What virtues have characterized the lives of the candidates before this campaign? The American public has a duty to inquire and a right to know.

*4. Pragmatism and Principle.* In politics, many of the day-to-day issues boil down to a matter of pragmatics. There are, after all, lots of different ways to skin the cat. People of good will can, and often will, disagree on the best way to address a large number of problems. Some issues, however, beg for a principled approach. Abortion is one example. Euthanasia is another. Embryonic stem cell research is a third. These issues involve profound questions about human rights and human dignity. The right to life should not be subject to being negotiated away in a backroom deal. Unless the right to life is protected, all other rights are meaningless. The right to worship, speak, or assemble as one pleases means nothing to a corpse. Sizing up one's stand on the right to life should be an important consideration in the assessment of any candidate.

*5. The Role of Religion.* Article VI of the Constitution provides that, " . . . no religious test shall ever be required as a qualification for any office or public trust under the United States." That does not mean, however, that a candidate's religious beliefs are irrelevant. Because religion is so fundamental to a person's character, it is an important factor to consider when evaluating a candidate. Religious faith affords a source of strength that transcends one's own resources. It can be an anchor that keeps one grounded through the difficult and depressing days that face any president. A solid foundation in Christian thought may have other positive effects. The Christian religion has been at the heart of Western culture and political thought for hundreds of years. Self-evident truths, equal protection under the law, separation of powers—all are grounded in the teaching of the Christian religion. Christian thought teaches that we have obligations not to just ourselves, but others also—including the weak and defenseless. While one's religion is relevant, we must keep in mind that we are electing a president, not a preacher. There is a difference—and we should not forget it. In the coming days, much discussion will center on the religious beliefs of can-

# Obama on Religion and Politics

For some time now, there has been plenty of talk among pundits and pollsters that the political divide in this country has fallen sharply along religious lines. Indeed, the single biggest "gap" in party affiliation among white Americans today is not between men and women, or those who reside in so-called Red States and those who reside in Blue, but between those who attend church regularly and those who don't.

Conservative leaders have been all too happy to exploit this gap, consistently reminding evangelical Christians that Democrats disrespect their values and dislike their Church, while suggesting to the rest of the country that religious Americans care only about issues like abortion and gay marriage; school prayer and intelligent design.

Democrats, for the most part, have taken the bait. At best, we may try to avoid the conversation about religious values altogether, fearful of offending anyone and claiming that—regardless of our personal beliefs—constitutional principles tie our hands. At worst, there are some liberals who dismiss religion in the public square as inherently irrational or intolerant, insisting on a caricature of religious Americans that paints them as fanatical, or thinking that the very word "Christian" describes one's political opponents, not people of faith.

*Barack Obama,*
*Call to Renewal Keynote Address,*
*June 28, 2006.*

didates. The differences between Christianity, Mormonism, and Islam will be under scrutiny. Ideas really do have consequences, and belief impacts behavior. Therefore, the discussion of religion in public life is not only appropriate, but necessary. One can only hope that the discussion will be thoughtful and civil rather than rancorous and inflammatory.

These are just a few of the criteria that Americans will do well to consider in selecting their next president. It's an important choice. Nothing less than the future of our country and the fate of the free world is at stake.

> *"It is deeply troubling when religion is no longer just an element in understanding the character of a candidate but becomes a central part of a party's efforts to win votes or to pander to a certain religious group or constituency."*

# Political Candidates Rely Too Much on Religion

**Abraham H. Foxman**

*Abraham H. Foxman is an author and the national director of the Anti-Defamation League. In the following viewpoint, he discerns a trend toward more aggressive and excessive professions of religious faith by political candidates, which he argues can be divisive and unhealthy for the nation. Foxman suggests that political candidates should not have to pander to religious groups, and he believes that voters should focus on candidates' qualifications for office rather than on their religious beliefs.*

As you read, consider the following questions:

1. According to Foxman, what were the titles of some of the panels at the 2008 Democratic National Convention in Denver?

2. According to the author, what answer should a political candidate give when a debate moderator asks about his or her relationship with God?

3. How does Foxman characterize John F. Kennedy's speech on religion in 1960?

The political campaign season is now in high gear as the curtain falls on the Democrats in Denver and the Republicans in Minneapolis-St. Paul [at their respective political conventions in 2008].

While much of the media's focus has been on handicapping the candidates and their chances in November, we would like to call attention to one less-publicized aspect of the U.S. political scene in 2008, which we find troubling.

This year, there have been increasing signs that the presidential race will present the American public with a profoundly unsettling infusion of religion and religiosity.

The trend toward this growing insertion of faith into the presidential race was first evident in Denver, and then equally so in the Twin Cities.

## Signs of Trouble

At the Democratic National Convention, the program included panels on "How an Obama Administration Will Engage People of Faith," "Moral Values Issues Abroad," "Getting Out the Faith Vote" and "Common Ground on Common Good."

Members of the clergy from across the religious spectrum had a significant presence, conducting Scripture readings at a multifaith "kickoff event" and offering invocations and benedictions. There was a clear effort to be interdenominational, but it was also apparent that the Democrats felt compelled to infuse religion into their convention in order to be politically viable.

At the Republican convention, religiously themed events played a prominent role as well. Members of the clergy led the convention in prayer each day, and there was considerable time devoted to discussing subjects such as "faith-based initiatives and family values," which one Republican spokeswoman recently identified as being "at the heart of our party."

There was less focus on religious diversity and less of an effort to call public attention to the convention's religious content, probably because it was less of a departure from past Republican programs.

## Religious Expression Becomes Excessive

In raising our concerns, we mean no disrespect to religion or to family values. But there comes a point when being open about faith crosses a subtle line into pandering.

Some of what we have been seeing in this campaign is excessive and aggressive. It goes beyond a candidate's discussing how religion shapes his or her worldview. Rather, it's saying, "Vote for me because I'm a person of faith"—and that is directly contrary to the constitutional principle that there shall be no religious test for public office.

Both parties seem to have reached the conclusion that appealing to religious voters is good politics. But what kind of message does it send, in our religiously diverse society, when the two major presidential candidates sit in a church and forthrightly answer Pastor Rick Warren's questions about their personal relationship with Jesus?

Renewed faith-based initiatives, religious outreach teams and religious programming at the conventions all work to curry favor with those who care which party is most favorable toward the religious.

This may be good politics, but it is not healthy for our nation.

## Sending a Dangerous Message

This is not to say that Americans should oppose candidates who are religious, or that candidates shouldn't feel free to discuss their religious beliefs with the body politic. It is understandable that candidates, from time to time, will want to express their religious beliefs—and how their faith will inform and influence their policymaking. And there's nothing wrong with a candidate expressing his or her religious perspective—especially when confronted with misinformation, innuendo and rumor.

However, appealing to voters along religious lines can be divisive, and it is certainly contrary to the American ideal of including all Americans in the political process.

It is deeply troubling when religion is no longer just an element in understanding the character of a candidate but becomes a central part of a party's efforts to win votes or to pander to a certain religious group or constituency. Government should not endorse, promote, or subsidize religious views—and particular religious views should not be the determining factor in public-policy decision making.

Anyone who legitimately aspires to public office in the United States must be prepared to set an example and to be a leader for all Americans, no matter his or her faith, or whether he or she even has a faith.

## Qualifications Should Be Paramount

When candidates campaign, they should be encouraging voters to make decisions based on an assessment of their qualifications, their integrity and their political positions, not on how religious they are.

The next time a debate moderator asks the candidates to discuss their personal relationship with God, it would be refreshing to hear an answer similar to the one President Kennedy gave nearly 48 years ago, when he confronted questions about his Catholicism: "I am not the Catholic candidate for president. I am the Democratic Party's candidate for president who happens also to be a Catholic."

Religion, he was saying, is part of him, but it does not define him, and it should not be the primary lens through which Americans view him.

In this season, it is important to remind all political players that in this religiously diverse nation, there is a point at which an emphasis on religion in a political campaign becomes inappropriate and even unsettling.

# Periodical and Internet Sources Bibliography

*The following articles have been selected to supplement the diverse views presented in this chapter.*

| | |
|---|---|
| Stephen I. Adler and Karen E. Gross | "There Cannot Be a Religious Litmus Test to Hold Public Office," *Austin (TX) American-Statesman*, November 30, 2010. |
| Peter Beinart | "The Jesus Litmus Test," *Daily Beast*, July 15, 2010. |
| Neal Gabler | "Politics as Religion in America," *Los Angeles Times*, October 2, 2009. |
| Phil Lawler | "Church-State Relations: A Wall of Separation or a One-Way Street?," CatholicCulture.org, May 12, 2010. www.catholicculture.org. |
| Roland S. Martin | "Democrats Finally Getting Religion on Religion," CNN.com, April 8, 2008. www.cnn.com. |
| Nedra Pickler | "Obama: Don't Give Religious Litmus Test," *Christian Post*, September 10, 2008. |
| Robert D. Putnam and David E. Campbell | "Walking Away from Church," *Los Angeles Times*, October 17, 2010. |
| Alan Reynolds | "Politics and Religion," *Washington Times*, February 18, 2007. |
| Tim Rutten | "Hate Under Cloak of Religion," *Los Angeles Times*, December 10, 2010. |
| Z. Byron Wolf | "Stained-Glass Ceiling: Would America Vote for a Non-Christian?," ABCNews.com, August 20, 2010. www.abcnews.go.com. |

OPPOSING
VIEWPOINTS®
SERIES

CHAPTER 3

# How Does the Separation of Church and State Impact Policy Decisions?

# Chapter Preface

In 2008 a wildly controversial California proposition was placed on the state ballot. Proposition 8—more commonly known as Prop 8—proposed a constitutional amendment that would overturn a California Supreme Court decision that just weeks before had allowed same-sex marriage. Prop 8 provided that "only marriage between a man and a woman is valid or recognized in California." It did not, however, affect domestic partnerships in the state or same-sex marriages performed before November 5, 2008. More than 52 percent of California voters voted for Prop 8, which effectively ended the practice of same-sex marriage in the state.

One of the more controversial aspects of Prop 8 was the role of religious organizations in the campaign for the ballot measure. Although some religious organizations opposed it, such as a number of Jewish groups, others provided key financial support, advocacy, and outreach to get it passed. Supporters included the Roman Catholic Church, evangelical Christians, orthodox Jewish groups, and the Eastern Orthodox Church. All of these groups endorsed the measure and were vocal about their opposition to same-sex marriage, arguing that such unions would condone homosexuality and redefine marriage, which would be against their religious beliefs. For many religious people, heterosexual marriage is an essential institution and should not be changed.

But it was the heavy involvement of the Church of Jesus Christ of Latter-Day Saints (LDS) that became one of the most controversial aspects of the campaign. The Mormon Church provided an invaluable source of financial donations in support of Prop 8, which were funneled through Protect Marriage.com, the official website of the group supporting the ballot measure. In fact, ProtectMarriage.com estimates that about half the donations they received came from LDS sources, and that 80 to 90 percent of the early volunteers who went door-to-door to advocate for the policy were LDS members. Even more controversial was the fact that much of the money—about 45 percent of out-of-state contributions to ProtectMarriage.com—came from Utah where LDS is based. It has been estimated that Mormon church members contributed approximately $20 million to the campaign overall. Much of that money was put directly into television commercials, which blanketed the California airwaves in the weeks before the election.

With such significant involvement from a religious group, especially with much of the financial backing coming from out-of-state, the issue erupted in controversy. Opponents of Prop 8 accused the LDS Church of violating church and state principles, arguing that the LDS participation in the campaign was a blatant attempt to impose their religious views on the state. Supporters of Prop 8 defended LDS involvement, underscoring the rights of individuals to express themselves within the parameters of the law. After all, it was California citizens—not Utah citizens—who turned out and voted to outlaw same-sex marriage.

On August 14, 2010, US district chief justice Vaughn Walker overturned Prop 8. That decision is on appeal, so the fate of same-sex marriage in California is still undecided.

The role of religious organizations in Prop 8 is just one of the topics examined in the following chapter, which considers how the separation of church and state affects policy decisions. Other subjects covered in the chapter include the ban on embryonic stem cell research, the immigration debate, and school vouchers.

*"The faith-based movement has become louder and more active in calling for what they describe as a 'humane' immigration overhaul."*

# Religious Leaders Are Becoming More Active in Immigration Debate

## Cindy Carcamo

*Cindy Carcamo is a reporter for California's* Orange County Register. *In the following viewpoint, she chronicles the movement launched by religious leaders to push for a comprehensive and compassionate immigration reform policy. Carcamo discerns a divide, however, between religious leaders and many of their parishioners, who do not often support such policies.*

As you read, consider the following questions:

1. As stated by the author, how have many faith-based organizations come together to address the issue of immigration reform?

2. Why is there a heightened level of activism on the issue of immigration reform, according to Carcamo?

3. What document did religious groups from Lutherans to Jewish congregations sign, as reported by the author?

Many faith-based organizations have traditionally served as a first stop for immigrants—legal and illegal—who need help navigating American society.

Church leaders have held prayer vigils and recited lines of Scripture, telling their congregants the Bible preaches compassion for strangers. And they've offered educational and support services, in some cases providing a safe haven for those in the country illegally, and advocated independently for the rights of strangers in a foreign land.

## Taking It to the Next Level

Lately, however, religious leaders across the country have launched a more aggressive movement. On the heels of immigration reform legislation introduced last month [December 2009], the faith-based movement has become louder and more active in calling for what they describe as a "humane" immigration overhaul.

Leaders from predominantly immigrant churches and mainstream churches—including [the Southern Californian cities of] Costa Mesa and Santa Ana—are sharing ideas about how best to help non-immigrant congregants better understand and empathize with those in the country illegally. They've taken pilgrimages, circulated petitions and met with decision makers in Washington, D.C.

"If your faith is Biblically based it's not easy to ignore the scripture about welcoming thy neighbor, loving thy enemy," said the Rev. Alexia Salvatierra, a Lutheran pastor who will take part in a nationwide immigration reform vigil scheduled for Jan. 26 [2010].

Salvatierra, who oversees the Orange County chapter of Clergy and Laity United for Economic Justice, often travels from Los Angeles to Orange County to set up meetings with religious leaders from immigrant and non-immigrant congregations.

## Questions About Efficacy

Some, however, are skeptical about how effective this new faith-based push for immigration reform will be, and they question how it will translate from the pulpit to the halls of power in Washington, D.C. A recent study shows a disconnect between active faith leaders and parishioners who may not want to follow. Even some church leaders express conflicting emotions on how far they should take politicking during sermons.

This heightened activism is partly due to the highly publicized immigration workplace enforcement raids that took place across the country during the [George W. Bush] administration, said Sam Folwood, a senior fellow at the Center for American Progress, a liberal Washington, D.C. group.

"When they see it on television . . . these raids, I think it affects people," said Folwood, who wrote a report titled "Loving Thy Neighbor: Immigration Reform and Communities of Faith." "I think they became aware when they saw what was happening to people in their communities. When they saw the raids or those detained, when they saw families torn apart and children being pulled away."

Those actions sparked an awakening in people of faith who lived in and around those communities and galvanized them to take action, he said.

In 2008, religious groups ranging from Lutherans to Jewish congregations signed an "Interfaith Statement in Support of Comprehensive Immigration Reform."

## Divide Between Pulpit and Parishioners?

Rabbi Arnold Rachlis, who heads University Synagogue in Irvine, said he's spoken about the issue of immigration—legal and illegal—since he first took the helm 18 years ago.

"Nothing defines a Jew more or should define a Jew more than empathy for those in the margins of society. . . . We know what it's like to wander from country to country," Rachlis said.

While he may preach empathy for those in the country illegally, Rachlis said his job is to provide guidance and to educate, not to push his congregants to take a certain political action.

"I think that's inappropriate and in some cases illegal," he said. "I would never from the pulpit endorse a political bill or particular action. I think it's presumptuous. . . . You want to encourage people to know and understand issues. You really leave it up to them to take the action they deem correct."

While some religious leaders may be vocal in pushing for immigration reform, congregants may not necessarily follow, according to a report released [in December 2009] by the Center for Immigration Studies, an anti–illegal immigration group in Washington, D.C.

"Religious Leaders vs. Members: An Examination of Contrasting Views on Immigration" contends that while national religious leaders lobby for immigration reform, individuals who belong to the same religious communities strongly support reducing overall immigration.

"That's what makes the issue always so contentious," said Steven Camarota, the study's author. "The top people in the church—as in the unions and in any set of organizations you care to name—and the rank and file have a different perspective."

## Religious Leaders Are Out of Touch

Religious leaders are possibly out of touch with the struggles of some of their blue-collar, lower-skilled parishioners who may be competing with illegal workers for jobs, Camarota said.

## A Moral Issue

Finally, what is the ultimate moral issue in [the immigration] debate that we want to highlight? Well, there are several, of course, and we see it every day: separation of families, exploitation in the workplace, deaths in the desert. But the ultimate moral issue is do we want to live in a country where we have a permanent underclass? Where we have a system which expropriates the work and taxes of human beings but does not offer them the protection of the law? I think the American public would say no because it undermines our values of fairness, opportunity, and compassion in this country which has really served our nation over the last 200 years. And I firmly believe that working together, the faith groups will lead the American public to that conclusion and that they will say that immigration reform is the answer.

*Kevin Appleby,*
*"Religious Acitivism and the Debate over Immigration Reform,"*
*Brookings Institution, June 15, 2010.*

"It's a class question," he said. "The leadership of these organizations is from the top of the social classes, usually. . . . Most of the people who head these organizations are college-educated, and in a way project from their personal experiences."

The report's findings were based on a poll conducted by Zogby International, which was commissioned by the center. The poll was conducted in November [2009] as an online survey of 42,026 adults, made up of people who described themselves as Catholic, mainline Protestant, born-again Protestant or Jewish. The margin of error is 0.5 percent.

Folwood and some faith leaders, however, took issue with the center's report, saying the questions were designed in a limited fashion, especially when respondents were asked about the cause of the 11 to 12 million people who are believed to be in the country illegally.

Folwood said his report shows that the faith-based immigration reform movement is fueled by congregants.

"So many peoples' faiths are in favor of comprehensive immigration reform," he said. "It's coming from the grassroots that's pushing leadership on the issue."

## From Rhetoric to Action

Immigrant rights activists are hoping that the non-immigrant faithful with a common belief in compassion will get a new perspective on the immigration issue—especially about those in the country illegally—that will compel them into action.

Orange County immigration advocates reached out to religious leaders in immigrant communities in 2007 but it soon became clear that was not effective by itself, said Salvatierra of the Clergy and Laity United for Economic Justice.

Ten Orange County congregations, including The Crossing Church in Costa Mesa, have already committed to informal meetings with pastors who lead immigrant churches, such as Templo Calvario in Santa Ana, said Wendy Tarr, a local coordinator with Salvatierra's group.

The organization is looking to launch a ministry that will give non-immigrant congregants the opportunity to visit children who are in immigration detention so they can put a face to the overall immigration issue, she said.

"The point is to expose people to the brokenness of the system they are hearing about," Tarr said.

## A Deep Topic

While congregants may have a better opportunity to see the human face behind those who enter the country illegally, it remains unclear whether they will be compelled to take action.

Shawn Scott, who is on staff at Rock Harbor Church in Costa Mesa, said he didn't think much about the issue of immigration until he served in a ministry that helped tutor low-income children—some who belonged to immigrant families.

Scott said the ministry helped him put a face to a complex issue but it didn't help him understand it any better.

He's far from calling his representative, demanding immigration reform.

"I can't push for it one way or another," he said. "It's such a deep topic."

> "Liberal leaders and Catholic bishops
> are seeing their flocks dwindle and im-
> migration presents an unprecedented
> recruiting opportunity."

# Religious Leaders' Immigration Activism Is a Political Convenience

## Benjamin Van Horrick

*Benjamin Van Horrick is a researcher at the National Journal-
ism Center. In the following viewpoint, Van Horrick singles out
Roman Catholic religious leaders for violating the rule of law by
advocating for illegal immigrants. He points out that Democrats
usually tell Catholic clergy to stay out of politics, but he suggests
that these Democrats have violated their own commitment to
the separation of church and state in order to have Catholic support for illegal immigrants. Van Horrick argues that this support
of Catholics is for political convenience only, since liberals have
not changed their views on other social issues, such as abortion.
Van Horrick also argues that advocating the breaking of the law
is not a good strategy for the Catholic Church and that there are
better ways to make its influence felt in the immigration debate.*

Benjamin Van Horrick, "Illegal Immigration Unites Democrats, Catholic Church?,"
*Human Events*, June 21, 2006. Copyright © 2006 by *Human Events*. Reproduced by permission.

As you read, consider the following questions:

1. What advice did the US Conference of Catholic Bishops give that earned them Democratic support, according to the author?

2. List two social issues about which liberals, according to Van Horrick, have not followed Catholic teaching?

3. According to the author, how might the Catholic Church better address the illegal immigration issue?

Catholic bishops shouldn't talk about politics, left-wing pundits say, except on the subject of illegal immigration. On that subject even the most ardent supporters of the separation of church and state are happy to hear the bishops opine. Liberals are cheering the U.S. Conference of Catholic Bishops for calling on churchgoers to harbor illegal immigrants in their homes to keep them safe from the U.S. Border Patrol.

On Ash Wednesday, Cardinal Roger Mahoney of Los Angeles instructed priests and churchgoers to disobey enforcement provisions of a House of Representatives immigration bill. Washington, D.C., Cardinal Theodore McCarrick said the scriptures justified aiding illegal immigrants. McCarrick said, "[How] many of us have not violated some laws, whatever they might have been—either they're traffic laws or immigration laws or tax laws, something like that."

Sen. Hillary Clinton (D.-N.Y.) recently said that immigration enforcement would make "Jesus himself" a criminal. She compared the plight of illegal immigrants to the Good Samaritan from the Gospels. However, her ham-handed attempts to co-opt religion for political gain has yielded conflicting results. She flatly rejects the position taken in the Bible on other social issues such as abortion and gay rights. She strangely remarked to the Richmond [VA] *Times-Dispatch* in 1997, "I have to confess that it's crossed my mind that you could not be a Republican and a Christian."

Politics does make strange bedfellows. The Democratic activists overlook their criticism of the church's social conservatism. But if liberals embraced the entirety of the church's influence, the American political landscape would be much different. Feminists would not take to the streets to tell the clergy to get their "rosary beads off my uterus." Liberal lawmakers would have praised Catholics who spoke out against the death-by-starvation of Terri Schiavo.[1] Senate Democrats would not question how the Catholic faith of Supreme Court nominees John Roberts and Sam Alito might affect their judicial decisions. The left-leaning media wouldn't defend pro-abortion Catholics when they were denied communion by Catholic bishops for breaking with Catholic doctrine on abortion. But we know better. Liberals will support the church when it's only politically convenient.

This is a marriage of political convenience for the church as well. Liberal leaders and Catholic bishops are seeing their flocks dwindle and immigration presents an unprecedented recruiting opportunity. The church is looking for new members. The Democratic Party needs new voters, proven by its lack of electoral success since 1994.

Still, the synergy between these two recent foes creates a dilemma for each. The church is excusing criminal violations of immigration law, while attempting to explain their former intransigence during investigation into alleged pedophile priests. Democrats have a record of criticizing the church for entering into public affairs and they are trying to have it both ways. It might backfire. Both face further erosion of their base, in light of championing amnesty for lawbreakers.

No one is saying that the Catholic Church should not speak out when politics and morality overlap, such as on the

1. Terri Schiavo, in a vegetative state for fifteen years, was taken off life support at the request of her husband but against the wishes of her parents. After an intense court battle, Schiavo's husband's wishes prevailed and in 2005 she died of starvation and dehydration.

death penalty and the plight of the poor. The church has long been one of the most effective voices for America's most vulnerable.

But when the church condones the illegal harboring of immigrants, it invites criticism even from its friends. While the church has been accused of blocking criminal investigations of their priests, it is hardly the right time to call for wholesale lawbreaking in the name of immigration rights.

The use of the illegal immigration issue comes at a high price for each party. Catholics, many of whom are the children or grandchildren of legal immigrants, may lose respect for their church for excusing law breaking.

The church has a way out. Catholic bishops could amend their statements and come out in favor of increasing legal immigration. Parishes could sponsor immigrants seeking citizenship by providing civic education, living assistance and moral substance. If they choose not to take this track, churchgoers and others may well consider the bishops less as a beacon of moral authority and more as political actors. That would not be a step in the right direction.

The civil rights movement succeeded with the help of the church by encouraging the reform of laws, not breaking them. The bishops should do the same today–or they risk polarizing themselves in a nation increasingly divided over immigration.

> "The approval of a constitutional ban on gay marriage raises troubling but age-old issues concerning the lines between religion and government."

# Proposition 8 Violates the Separation of Church and State

## James Brosnahan

*James Brosnahan is an author and lawyer. In the following viewpoint, he maintains that Proposition 8, which denies gays and lesbians the right to marry in California, violates the separation of church and state. Brosnahan notes that the supporters of Proposition 8 were motivated by religious beliefs and succeeded in forcing them on all Californians. He predicts there will be a challenge under the US Constitution because discrimination is unlawful.*

As you read, consider the following questions:

1. In what year did Proposition 8 pass, as reported by Brosnahan?

James Brosnahan, "Church and State: The Issue of Prop. 8," SFGate.com, November 9, 2008. Copyright © 2008 by SFGate.com. Reproduced by permission.

2. How did the US Supreme Court rule on a California constitutional amendment that limited fair housing in the 1960s, according to the author?

3. According to Brosnahan, how has marriage been used as a method of oppression in the past?

Proposition 8 has passed, denying to some the right enjoyed by other citizens in California, the right to marry. Now, the central question for the courts to decide is: Are gays in California equal, or can members of certain churches declare them constitutionally inferior?

The approval of a constitutional ban on gay marriage raises troubling but age-old issues concerning the lines between religion and government. Before the founders of our country separated church and state, there were hundreds of years of turmoil caused by one religion dominating the government and using it against nonbelievers.

In the aftermath of Tuesday's [November 4, 2008,] vote, do gays and lesbians in California have a reason to believe that they have been abused, discriminated against and relegated to a separate-but-equal status?

## The Fight Continues

Yes, and that's why this fight is far from over. There will be a challenge under the U.S. Constitution. In the 1960s, the U.S. Supreme Court struck down a California constitutional amendment that limited fair housing on the grounds that prejudice could not be put into a state Constitution.

No one can forecast the outcome of this next fight, but there is bound to be some fallout that may harm those religions that so vehemently insisted that their beliefs be placed in the California Constitution. All religions require tolerance to flourish, but in Proposition 8 some religious groups aimed at and wounded gay people in California.

The drafters of the U.S. Constitution had a brilliant, experienced view concerning the importance of drawing the lines to protect religion on the one hand and civil government on the other. They put those lines in the First Amendment to the U.S. Constitution. Today, those lines are very relevant.

Government may not attack religion. Californians who have religious beliefs concerning the proper scope of marriage may exercise those rights as they see fit. Churches have always been able to proceed as they wish concerning marriage ceremonies. There was no mandate to suppress religious beliefs. This should be obvious to everyone in California because of our tolerance of all religions.

## Forcing Religious Beliefs on Everyone

That the supporters of Proposition 8 were motivated by religious beliefs cannot be denied. Now the religious beliefs of some Californians are in our Constitution and, until overturned, govern us all whether we like it or not.

The other branch of the First Amendment is equally important. The state may not establish a religion. The state may not take principles of religious belief from a religion, any religion, and establish it as the law applicable to all. This line establishing the double branch of protection of religion on the one hand and no establishment on the other was arrived at after hundreds of years of turmoil.

Historically, marriage was used as a method of oppressing a despised group. These lessons of history are relevant to reflect on today. In Ireland, for 150 years, the penal laws provided that no Protestant could marry a Catholic.

Much more recent in the United States were the rules against marriage between a black person and a white person. These were struck down by the U.S. Supreme Court in the 1960s and the California Supreme Court in the 1940s. Using the civil marriage ceremony as a method of expressing gov-

"Gay Marriage," cartoon by Pat Bagley. Copyright © 2010 by Pat Bagley, *Salt Lake Tribune*, and www.PoliticalCartoons.com. All rights reserved.

ernmental disdain toward a particular group is as old as the Sierra Nevada. It has been an assault on tolerance.

## Marriage Is a Fundamental Right

Finally, marriage is a fundamental right in constitutional analysis. There are very few things in life more important than the ability to choose one's partner. Marriage is not just a word; it is a status, a state of mind, a way of being. Look in any direction and you will see examples of the people's respect for the institution of marriage.

A large group of Californians has now been denied that fundamental institution. These folks are our neighbors, our friends, our colleagues and our relatives. The constitutional promise of this state is, as the California Supreme Court held, that they are equally protected in the enjoyment of rights by all Californians. But the voters have spoken.

Now it will be up to the courts to explain whether equality is real—or just an illusion. I would not wish to be the one to justify this vote to a gay woman going to Afghanistan in the military, to a gay police officer who risks everything so we may be safe or any of the other thousands of gays and lesbians in California who contribute so much to our culture, our advancement and our well being.

I cannot square this vote with my view that Californians are decent, accepting and tolerant. But I know that the gays and lesbians of California, like the oppressed Catholics of Ireland who lived under penal laws, will fight this visible, constitutional, embarrassing injustice until it is no more. And when that day comes, we will live in a better state.

> "The First Amendment was not intended
> to prohibit religious participation in
> political life, and it certainly does not
> mandate that only the morals of the
> non-church-attenders are constitution-
> ally permissible bases of legislation."

# Proposition 8 Does Not Violate the Separation of Church and State

*Robert Alt*

*Robert Alt is a lawyer and the senior legal fellow and deputy di-
rector of the Center for Legal and Judicial Studies at the Heritage Foundation, a conservative Washington, D.C., think tank.
In the following viewpoint, Alt dismisses allegations that Proposition 8, which denies gays and lesbians the right to marry in
California, violates the separation of church and state. Alt contends that such charges reveal an antireligious bias on the part
of accusers and points out that American law always has been
influenced by religious belief and theology.*

Robert Alt, "Still Stoned Out of His Mind," *National Review Online*, November 20, 2008.
NationalReview.com. Copyright © 2008 by *National Review Online*. Reproduced by permission.

As you read, consider the following questions:

1. When did the California Supreme Court decide to hear arguments concerning the legality of Proposition 8, according to Alt?

2. Why does the author believe the arguments made "pretty thin gruel"?

3. What did Geoff Stone use for proof that Proposition 8 was a violation of church-state separation, according to Alt?

The California Supreme Court Wednesday [November 17, 2008,] decided to hear arguments concerning the legality of Proposition 8, which amended the state Constitution to restore marriage to what it was before the California Supreme Court engaged in legal adventurism by creating a right to gay marriage.

The arguments made are pretty thin gruel, and turn on a technical question of whether the change should be an amendment, which can be passed (as Prop. 8 was) by a majority vote of the people after collecting enough signatures to qualify for the ballot, or whether it is such a drastic change that it needed to go through the more arduous process of constitutional revision. Deep down, some of the lawyers making these arguments had to find it ironic to argue that the state Constitution could not be modified to change the right to marriage through the formal amendment process, including the approval of a majority of voters, but that it could be done by four judges who changed the law by their own fiat. The case law is pretty strongly against those challenging Prop. 8, enough so that I think even the California Supreme Court will have trouble legislating ... oops, I mean carefully legally reasoning their way to the conclusion that Prop. 8 is unlawful.

## The Right to Free Speech

The contention that religious people cannot advocate religiously based moral views as public policy is simply censorship. The bedrock of the American constitution is full and free public debate of issues. By all means, let the debate be civil and without rancor, but no one's views of what is moral or sound policy deserves to be silenced!

*Alan J. Reinach, Church State Council, 2008.*

## Charges of Constitutional Violation

Enter Geoff Stone [Edward H. Levi Distinguished Service Professor of Law at the University of Chicago]. Before the Court opted to hear the case, he suggested that there was really a much bigger constitutional issue at play here: the separation of church and state. He finds that Proposition 8 "enact[s] into law a particular religious belief." For Stone, religion is the only explanation for the law: "Indeed, despite invocations of tradition, morality and family values, it seems clear that the only honest explanation for Proposition 8 is religion." His proof: polling data which shows that evangelicals and weekly church attenders favored Prop. 8 by large margins, while non-Christians and non-church-attenders opposed it. While he concedes that courts are loathe to intervene in these cases, it is clear that he thinks they should. Indeed, to allow these kind of laws is "un-American", as he explains with perfect tone-deaf deftness: "Indeed, regardless of whether courts can intervene in this context, it is as un-American to violate the separation of church and state by using the power of the state to impose our religious beliefs on others as it is to use the power of the state to impose our discriminatory views of race, religion or gender on others."

Where to begin? Should we talk about the fact that a traditional head of the police powers of the state are morals, which often were derived from the religious sentiments of the people? Should we discuss the role of religious law like the Decalogue [Ten Commandments] in shaping much of American law? Should we dispute the correlation between religious voters and religious enactments, noting that weekly church attenders also vote overwhelmingly for other things that Geoff Stone no doubt despises, like Republican party presidential candidates? Should we dispute the premise that "only" religion explains the outcome in the election, and that people of very different religious faiths and no faith at all reached the same conclusion in voting for Prop. 8? No, to do so gives Stone too much credit. His arguments don't even qualify as reasonable fringe in establishment clause jurisprudence.

## Foolish Arguments

One might wish to dismiss his blog post simply as a poorly thought out whim made on a Sunday afternoon, after church bells in Hyde Park [the Chicago neighborhood where the University of Chicago is located] somehow triggered dementia. But alas, Stone has a track record of these absurdly anti-religious rants to allow such a kind explanation. As Bench Memos readers will recall, he previously asserted that the court's decision upholding the federal partial-birth abortion statute was a result of a new Catholic majority on the Court. . . .

What then becomes obvious is that it is Stone who is acting with religious fervor by attempting to impose his religious, or if you prefer, irreligious beliefs or morality on the public square. The First Amendment was not intended to prohibit religious participation in political life, and it certainly does not mandate that only the morals of the non-church-attenders are constitutionally permissible bases of legislation.

But it is not suitable to claim that arguments like Stone's are "un-American," to borrow his line. They are simply foolish.

> *"To deprive scientists of the freedom to use clusters of cells to do [embryonic stem cell] research is to violate their rights—as well as the rights of all who would contribute to, invest in, or benefit from this research."*

# Banning Federal Funds for Embryonic Stem Cell Research Violates the Separation of Church and State

## David Holcberg and Alex Epstein

*David Holcberg is a media research specialist and Alex Epstein is a junior fellow at the Ayn Rand Institute. In the following viewpoint, they attribute political opposition to embryonic stem cell research to religious dogma, contending that pro-lifers are attempting to impose their religious views on the rest of the American people. Holcberg and Epstein argue that opponents of embryonic stem cell research are violating the rights of scientists doing the research and of the patients who need it for survival.*

David Holcberg and Alex Epstein, "The Anti-Life Opposition to Embryonic Stem Cell Research," AynRand.org, May 20, 2005. Copyright © 2005 by Ayn Rand Center for Individual Rights. Reproduced by permission.

As you read, consider the following questions:

1. How do the authors describe the embryos used in stem cell research?

2. What is the result of political pressure against embryonic stem cell research, according to Holcberg and Epstein?

3. According to the authors, what diseases can be helped by embryonic stem cell research?

It is widely known that embryonic stem cell research has the potential to revolutionize medicine and save millions of lives. Yet many Congressmen are frantically working to defeat a measure that would expand federal financing of this research. Why are they (and so many others) opposing embryonic stem cell research—and doing so under the banner of being "pro-life"?

The opponents of embryonic stem cell research claim that their position is rooted in "respect for human life." They say that the embryos destroyed in the process of extracting stem cells are human beings with a right to life.

But embryos used in embryonic stem cell research are manifestly not human beings—not in any rational sense of the term. These embryos are smaller than a grain of sand, and consist of at most a few hundred undifferentiated cells. They have no body or body parts. They do not see, hear, feel, or think. While they have the *potential* to become human beings—if implanted in a woman's uterus and brought to term—they are nowhere near *actual* human beings.

What, then, is the "pro-lifers'" reason for regarding these collections of cells as sacred and attributing rights to them? Religious dogma.

## Religion Intrudes on Science

The "pro-lifers" accept on faith the belief that rights are a divine creation: a gift from an unknowable supernatural being bestowed on embryos at conception (which many extend to embryos "conceived" in a beaker). The most prominent example of this view is the official doctrine of the Catholic Church, which declares to its followers that an embryo "is to be respected and treated as a person from the moment of conception; and therefore from that same moment his rights as a person must be recognized."

But rights are not some supernatural construct, mystically granted by the will of "God." They are this-worldly principles of proper political interaction rooted in man's rational nature. Rights recognize the fact that men can only live successfully and happily among one another if they are free from the initiation of force against them. Rights exist to protect and further human life. Rights enable individual men to think, act, produce and trade, live and love in freedom. The principle of rights is utterly inapplicable to tiny, prehuman clusters of cells that are incapable of such actions.

In fact, to attribute rights to embryos is to call for the violation of actual rights. Since the purpose of rights is to enable individuals to secure their well-being, a crucial right, inherent in the right to liberty and property, is the right to do scientific research in pursuit of new medical treatments. To deprive scientists of the freedom to use clusters of cells to do such research is to violate their rights—as well as the rights of all who would contribute to, invest in, or benefit from this research.

## People Need This Life-Saving Research

And to the extent that rights are violated in this way, we can expect deadly results. The political pressure against embryonic stem cell research is already discouraging many scientists and businessmen from investing their time and resources in its pursuit. If this research can lead, as scientists believe, to the ability to create new tissues and organs to replace damaged ones, any obstacles placed in its path will unnecessarily delay

## What Are Embryonic Stem Cells?

Embryonic stem cells, as their name suggests, are derived from embryos. Most embryonic stem cells are derived from embryos that develop from eggs that have been fertilized *in vitro*—in an *in vitro* fertilization clinic—and then donated for research purposes with informed consent of the donors. They are *not* derived from eggs fertilized in a woman's body.

*National Institutes of Health, 2010.*

the discovery of new cures and treatments for diseases such as Parkinson's, Alzheimer's, osteoporosis, and diabetes. Every day that this potentially life-saving research is delayed is another day that will go by before new treatments become available to ease the suffering and save the lives of countless individuals. And if the "pro-lifers" ever achieve the ban they seek on embryonic stem cell research, millions upon millions of human beings, living or yet to be born, might be deprived of healthier, happier, and longer lives.

The enemies of embryonic stem cell research know this, but are unmoved. They are brazenly willing to force countless human beings to suffer and die for lack of treatments, so that clusters of cells remain untouched.

To call such a stance "pro-life" is beyond absurd. Their allegiance is not to human life or to human rights, but to their anti-life dogma.

If these enemies of human life wish to deprive themselves of the benefits of stem cell research, they should be free to do so and die faithful to the last. But any attempt to impose their religious dogma on the rest of the population is both evil and unconstitutional. In the name of the actual sanctity of human life and the inviolability of rights, embryonic stem cell research must be allowed to proceed unimpeded. Our lives may depend on it.

> "Taxpayers should not have to foot the
> bill for experiments that require the
> destruction of human life."

# Taxpayers Should Not Be Forced to Fund Embryonic Stem Cell Research

**Warren Mass**

*Warren Mass is a contributing editor at* The New American. *In the following viewpoint, he contends that the 2009 reversal of the ban on federal funding for embryonic stem cell research revealed a disturbing lack of ethical consideration on the part of President Barack Obama's administration, even going so far as to draw a comparison to Adolf Hitler's view on the Jewish race. Mass argues that decisions on stem cell research funding should be left up to the states and that reversing the ban forces taxpayers to pay for morally repugnant research that is explicitly against their religious beliefs—which, he contends, is a gross violation of government authority.*

Warren Mass, "Obama Lifts Ban on Embryonic Stem-Cell Research," *The New American*, March 9, 2009. www.TheNewAmerican.com. Copyright © 2009 by *The New American*. Reproduced by permission.

As you read, consider the following questions:

1. When did President George W. Bush issue an executive order restricting federal funding of embryonic stem cell research, according to Mass?

2. According to the author, what does Tony Perkins believe the federal government should be funding instead of embryonic stem cell research?

3. Why does the author believe that funding should be a matter for the states?

President Barack Obama signed an executive order on March 9 [2009] that reverses the current ban on federal funding of human embryonic stem-cell research. The move overturns an August 9, 2001 executive order issued by President George W. Bush that restricted federal funding of embryonic stem-cell research to the existing 60 cell lines derived from human embryos destroyed long ago.

## Reversing the Ban

"Rather than furthering discovery, our government has forced what I believe is a false choice between sound science and moral values," said Obama. "In this case, I believe the two are not inconsistent. As a person of faith, I believe we are called to care for each other and work to ease human suffering. I believe we have been given the capacity and will to pursue this research and the humanity and conscience to do so responsibly."

The *Washington Post* quoted Melody C. Barnes, director of Obama's Domestic Policy Council, who said in a telephone interview on March 8: "The president believes that it's particularly important to sign this memorandum so that we can put science and technology back at the heart of pursuing a broad range of national goals."

The *Post* also quoted Harold Varmus, who co-chairs Obama's Council of Advisors on Science and Technology, as stating, "We view what happened with stem-cell research in the last administration as one manifestation of failure to think carefully about how federal support of science and the use of scientific advice occurs. This is consistent with the president's determination to use sound scientific practice, responsible practice of science and evidence, *instead of dogma in developing federal policy.*" (Emphasis added.)

Varmus added: "As a result of lifting those limitations, the president is in effect allowing federal funding of embryonic stem cell research to the extent it's permitted by federal law—that is, work with [human embryonic] stem cells themselves, not the derivation of those stem cells."

## Opposition to the Move

The announcement brought rapid comment from Rep. Eric Cantor, the number-two ranking Republican in the House, who said on CNN's "State of the Union" that the administration's priorities should be on employment, rather than funding for embryonic stem-cell research: "Frankly, federal funding of embryonic stem-cell research can bring on embryo harvesting, perhaps even human cloning that occurs. We don't want that. . . . And certainly that is something that we ought to be talking about, but let's take care of business first. People are out of jobs."

A report in the *Christian Post* observed: "Obama's intent to lift restrictions on the controversial type of stem-cell research has been known for some time and is even articulated as part of his administration's agenda on the White House's Website. The White House agenda item dealing with the subject states: "Advance Stem Cell Research: Support increased stem cell research. Allow greater federal government funding on a wider array of stem cell lines." Curiously, the item is listed under the category of "Technology," rather than other likely categories such as "Ethics," "Family," or "Health Care."

The *Christian Post* also quoted a statement issued by Tony Perkins, president of the Family Research Council: "I believe it is unethical to use human life, even young embryonic life, to advance science. While such research is unfortunately legal, taxpayers should not have to foot the bill for experiments that require the destruction of human life."

Perkins continued: "We should be increasing funding for adult stem-cell treatments, which have been used to treat patients for over 70 diseases and conditions, and we should fund the historic achievements in reprogramming ordinary skin cells into embryonic-like stem cells without compromising ethics by destroying life."

## A Lack of Ethical Consideration

Comments from members of the scientific community provided insight into the fact that traditional ethical concerns seem to have had negligible impact upon the thinking of many modern researchers. The AP [Associated Press] quoted Dr. George Daley of the Harvard Stem Cell Institute and Children's Hospital of Boston, who said: "I feel vindicated after eight years of struggle, and I know it's going to energize my research team."

When the question was raised as to whether the Obama decision would remove prohibitions on creating embryos specifically to harvest their stem cells—a matter still to be determined—Dr. Mark A. Kay, a researcher at Stanford University's School of Medicine, told the *Washington Post*: "*I don't personally have any problem creating embryos for embryonic stem cell research*. But if he decides that embryos that have already been created and are going to be discarded are the ones that would be used, that would be reasonable as well. *These things* exist and are going to be discarded. It's really mind-boggling to me *these things* are going to be discarded and scientists haven't been allowed to use them to do research." (Emphasis added.)

Dr. Kay's callous reference to human embryos, which theologians of many faiths believe to be human beings with human souls, as "these things" reminds this writer of a remark made by the notorious mass murderer, Adolf Hitler, in *Mein Kampf*: "Certainly the Jew is also a man, but the flea is also an animal."

A common theme among proponents of the Obama order—originating with Obama himself—is that his action will somehow remove "politics" from scientific research. The *New York Times*, for example, reported on March 9 [2009] that "Mr. Obama's announcement on Monday will be part of a broader initiative to make good on his pledge to separate science and politics." As with the phrase "separation of church and state," however, this new mantra, "separation of science and politics," reverses the true order of government as stated in our Constitution. Our Constitution serves primarily to insulate the people and states from too much government in Washington, yet these phrases (one trite, the other likely to become so) promote bigger, bolder, and more intrusive government.

## Misconstruing the First Amendment

The First Amendment's prohibition against Congress making laws respecting an establishment of religion was an obvious restriction against the United States having a Church-of-England-type established church—yet it has been misconstrued to give federal courts the power to interfere in matters that should be reserved to the states or the people.

Likewise, the Constitution does not give any power to Congress to appropriate funds for scientific research, nor to establish the National Institutes of Health (NIH), which will oversee the expenditure of these unconstitutional federal funds. In fact, the Constitution's sole reference to science, under Article I, Section 8, is to "promote the progress of science and useful arts, by securing for limited times to authors and inventors the exclusive right to their respective writings and discoveries."

In other words, the government is authorized to grant patent protection to scientists, nothing more.

## Leave Stem Cell Research to the States

From a constitutional point of view, therefore, stem-cell research is not a federal matter at all, whether we are speaking of funding it, legitimizing it, or prohibiting it. As with other issues of ethical concern governing human behavior, the matter should be left to the states.

It must be said, however, that given the serious ethical considerations of artificially bringing into existence what many people believe is a human life—for the purpose of experimenting upon and ultimately destroying that life—makes federal funding of such activity particularly onerous. It makes taxpayers pay for actions they find morally repugnant. The proponents of using federal funding for such research claim that the Obama order will result in a "separation of science and politics," but it does just the *opposite*. All federal funding must be approved by members of Congress, who are, by trade . . . politicians.

> *"Using governmental funds to support any sort of religious education or educational institution violates the First Amendment's Establishment Clause, which states that 'Congress shall make no law respecting an establishment of religion.'"*

# School Vouchers Violate the Separation of Church and State

*Miranda Hale*

*Miranda Hale is a contributor to the discussion website Exam iner.com. In the following viewpoint, she claims that governmentally funded school voucher programs are detrimental to communities because government funds should not be allowed to support any kind of religious education. Hale also points out that recent studies have shown that school voucher programs have failed to significantly improve student achievement. She argues that enabling school voucher programs to continue or allowing new ones to take root will harm underfunded public schools.*

As you read, consider the following questions:

1. According to the author, what did the Supreme Court rule on the establishment clause in 1947's *Everson v. Board of Education*?

2. As described by Hale, what did the Supreme Court rule regarding the relationship between government and religion in 1971's *Lemon v. Kurtzman*?

3. What is "the Lemon test", as explained by the author?

Governmentally funded school voucher programs have the potential to negatively affect every community that relies on public schools to educate its children. Allowing a parent to use a voucher to pay for their child's private school education not only diverts much-needed funds from public schools but also brings up the crucial issue of maintaining the separation of church and state. Using governmental funds to support any sort of religious education or educational institution violates the First Amendment's Establishment Clause, which states that ""Congress shall make no law respecting an establishment of religion."

## Vouchers Are Ineffective

In contrast to what some proponents of voucher programs assert, vouchers are not an effective way to increase school accountability or improve students' academic performance. Recent experiments with voucher programs (specifically in Washington, D.C.) have failed to produce any significant improvement in student achievement. School vouchers are only useful, then, in one manner: they provide a dangerous loophole through which religious institutions may receive governmental funding.

Multiple United States Supreme Court cases have been precedent-setting regarding the interpretation and the implementation of the Establishment Clause. One of the most relevant to the voucher debate is 1947's *Everson v. Board of Education*, regarding the legality and the constitutionality of a New Jersey law that permitted local school boards to reimburse private (almost entirely religious) schools the cost of transportation for students. Although The Court ruled in a 5-4 decision that the state's practices were not unconstitutional, this case also offered an opportunity for The Court to set forth a clear opinion on the Establishment Clause. One part of this opinion is directly relevant to the issue of school vouchers and sets clear legal precedent:

> No tax in any amount, large or small, can be levied to support any religious activities or institutions, whatever they may be called, or whatever form they may adopt to teach or practice religion.

Another precedent-setting case regarding the issue of school vouchers is 1971's *Lemon v. Kurtzman*, in which the Court ruled that the government is not permitted to "excessively entangle" with religion. This case overturned a Pennsylvania education act, which, at that time, permitted the state Superintendent of Public Instruction to reimburse private, primarily Catholic, schools for teacher salaries and various educational materials. The Court overturned the act, ruling that it was in violation of the Establishment Clause.

## The "Lemon Test"

The most important precedent created by this ruling was the "Lemon test," which established requirements for cases dealing with potential violations of the separation of church and state. If any one of the three requirements is violated, the governmental action in question is in violation of the Establishment Clause. These requirements are, as laid out by then Chief Justice [Warren] Burger in the Court's opinion on this case:

> First, the statute must have a secular legislative purpose; second, its principal or primary effect must be one that neither

advances nor inhibits religion ... finally, the statute must not foster "an excessive government entanglement" with religion.

[In the above-mentioned recent instance,] although 56 percent of all participating schools were faith-based (39 percent were part of the Catholic Archdiocese of Washington), 82 percent of the treatment group attended a faith-based school, with 59 percent of them attending the 22 participating Catholic parochial schools.

This indicates that religious institutions, specifically Catholic ones in this case, are receiving significant amounts of federal funding from this program. This is a clear violation of the Establishment Clause. In July of 2009, Bipartisan Senators introduced support for The Scholarships for Opportunity and Results (SOAR) Act, which, if passed, would give the D.C. Opportunity Scholarship Program a five-year extension.

## An Unacceptable Outcome

Results of most current research into the effectiveness of voucher programs show that vouchers do not significantly improve students' academic performance. Instead, what these programs *are* succeeding at is diverting much-needed governmental educational funds to private religious institutions. This does great harm to all public school students. Even more dangerous, though, are the current effects and potential future consequences of permitting voucher programs to violate the Establishment Clause.

Allowing voucher programs to continue will do nothing but harm our already underfunded public schools and force all taxpayers to fund religion and religious institutions. Neither outcome is acceptable and both do a great disservice to both the Constitution and to all American citizens.

> "Using vouchers at parochial schools would probably pass constitutional muster as long as the public funds are not used for instruction or other activities that are explicitly and primarily religious."

# School Vouchers Do Not Necessarily Violate the Separation of Church and State

*Larry M. Elkin*

*Larry M. Elkin is a certified public accountant. In the following viewpoint, he suggests that school vouchers are a wise use of taxpayers' money because they provide school choice and a higher-quality education at religious schools. Elkin argues that the government has no qualms about funding other programs that support religious groups, such as college aid programs and Medicare. For these reasons, Elkin maintains, charges that school vouchers violate the principle of church-state separation ring hollow.*

Larry M. Elkin, "Can Superman Rescue Parochial Schools?," *Yonkers Tribune*, September 28, 2010. www.YonkersTribune.typepad.com. Copyright © 2010 by Palisades Hudson Financial Group LLC. Reproduced by permission.

As you read, consider the following questions:

1. According to the author, what did New York City reportedly spend per student in its public schools in 2008?

2. According Elkins, for the cost of one year in a public school in New York City, how many students could have their tuition paid for at the Holy Spirit Catholic School in the Bronx?

3. How much does a Catholic school tuition cost per student, according to the author?

For more than 80 years, the Holy Spirit Catholic School in the Bronx has stood across the street from Public School [P.S.] 26.

I attended P.S. 26 in the 1960s, but for me, Holy Spirit might as well have been on Mars. I never set foot in the place. I only knew a few Holy Spirit students, and they all happened to be girls. They were older than me and were the sort of older girls who thought little boys required scientific study, like bacteria or bugs. I kept my distance.

Otherwise, the only time my world intersected that of Holy Spirit was at 2 p.m. every Wednesday. At that hour, most of the Catholic kids in my class were escorted across the street to Holy Spirit for religious instruction. I didn't really know what religious instruction meant. It certainly didn't dawn on me that the five hours a week I spent after school at the Hebrew Institute of University Heights was a form of religious instruction. I did know, however, that the women who taught my classes at the Hebrew Institute of University Heights were far, far scarier than the Holy Spirit girls. Abraham and Moses in person would have been less intimidating.

Looking back, I regret never getting to know more of the people who occupied Holy Spirit. It's not that I wish I had attended Catholic school—I don't—but I have come to respect the very serviceable education Catholic schools have delivered to students in places like the Bronx, where public schools have failed far too many children for far too long.

## Catholic Schools Are in Trouble

Now, however, it's unclear how many Catholic schools will be able to afford to keep their doors open to the next generation of students. Catholic schools across the country have been forced to close due to declining enrollment and lack of funds. So many have been shuttered in recent years that church leaders have started referring to the closing of schools as "the melancholy rite," *The New York Times* reports.

New York's archbishop, Timothy M. Dolan, has indicated that he may resort to dramatic restructuring to save the schools of his archdiocese, which includes the New York City boroughs of Manhattan, the Bronx and Staten Island, in addition to seven other counties in the state. Under Dolan's plan, funding for the schools would be centralized, instead of leaving each parish to support its own school. The archbishop would strategically eliminate numerous schools in order to ensure the survival of the remaining ones. "We must admit that the days of expecting a parish by itself to support its school are coming to an end," Dolan wrote in the archdiocesan newspaper, *Catholic New York*.

As Catholic schools close, families are left with less choice as to where to send their children. Nonsectarian private schools in New York City charge upwards of $30,000 per year per child, an impossible sum for working-class parents. Even Holy Spirit's current tuition of just under $4,000 for a single student (siblings get discounts) is a major burden for the families that live in my old neighborhood. When schools like Holy Spirit go away, public schools—and, in lucky districts, alternative charter schools—become the only options.

The desperation of many public school students and their families is portrayed in the film *Waiting for 'Superman'*.... Directed and co-written by Davis Guggenheim, whose credits include an Academy Award for [the global warming documentary] *An Inconvenient Truth*, the film depicts the efforts of five inner-city youngsters to beat the educational odds that are stacked against them.

## Spend Taxpayers' Money Wisely

Which gets me to a simple question: Are we spending enormous amounts of public money on education so we can have public schools, or so we can get children educated by any means necessary?

Cost-effective parochial schools are closing by the hundreds for lack of enough tuition-paying students, while we spend far more than those schools' tuition to keep students in public schools that don't work. This is fiscal and educational malpractice.

We could go a long way toward solving our inner-city education problem by providing publicly financed vouchers that those students could use to pay tuition at any school that meets state educational standards, including parochial schools.

In the 2008 fiscal year, New York City reported spending $17,696 per student in its public schools, according to a study by the Cato Institute. The Institute estimates that actual per student spending in New York City that year may have been more like $21,543. For the cost of educating one student in the public school system, the city could have paid tuition for four or five students at Holy Spirit.

The added enrollment that vouchers would provide could make an enormous difference to those schools. In the Archdiocese of New York, for example, Latinos make up a small percentage of parochial school students, although nearly half of the Catholics in the archdiocese are Hispanic. Dolan attributes this discrepancy to the difficulty many families have paying tuition ranging from about $3,000 to $6,000 a year.

# What Is School Choice?

School Choice is . . .

[A] common sense idea that gives every parent the power and freedom to choose their children's education.

Common Sense

It is immoral that the quality of schooling is based on the value and location of your home. School choice gives parents the freedom to choose a school based on its quality and their child's needs, not their home address.

Parent Power

Most people can't afford to pay twice for education, once in taxes and once in private school tuition. School choice gives parents financial power by letting them use public funds set aside for education to send their children to a public or private school of their choice.

Parent Freedom

In America, children are assigned to a school based on where their parents live. School choice gives parents the freedom to choose a school—public or private, near or far, religious or secular—that works best for their children regardless of where they live.

Great Education

Public education in America just isn't working anymore no matter what we try or how much we spend. School choice forces all schools—public and private—to offer the best education possible in order to recruit and retain students.

*The Foundation for Educational Choice, 2010.*

Providing these students with the opportunity to attend Catholic schools, should they choose to do so, could significantly bolster enrollment.

## Criticism of Vouchers

Many opponents of school vouchers argue that the First Amendment makes it impossible for taxpayers' money to be used to pay religious institutions to instruct children. It is, of course, true that public treasuries cannot pay for the religious portion of the program, but this need not prevent governments from paying for the other elements of students' education.

At the college level, all sorts of government programs already help students pay tuition at religiously affiliated institutions. We have no qualms about allowing government-financed programs like Medicare and Medicaid to pay for treatment at hospitals operated by religious groups. For that matter, we provide exemptions from federal and state income taxes, and from local property taxes, for churches, synagogues, mosques and temples, as well as the schools they operate. Using vouchers at parochial schools would probably pass constitutional muster as long as the public funds are not used for instruction or other activities that are explicitly and primarily religious. The fact that parents could use vouchers for schools affiliated with any sect, or with no sect, is probably enough to make them legally sound as well as practical. I'm sure we can handle the bookkeeping.

Vouchers are not going to solve all our education problems, and parochial schools are not the answer for every child. We are going to have to put a lot of diverse pieces together to solve our educational policy puzzle. Each time a school like Holy Spirit closes, we lose one of those pieces.

> *"Abandoning what every civilization for millennia has understood marriage to be would harm children and undermine religious freedom."*

# Repealing the Defense of Marriage Act Would Threaten Religious Freedom

*Ron Sider*

*Ron Sider is president of Evangelicals for Social Action and a professor at Palmer Seminary near Philadelphia. In the following viewpoint, he claims that repealing the Defense of Marriage Act (DOMA) and legalizing gay marriage on a federal level threatens religious freedom because religious organizations will be pressured to abandon their religious beliefs and accept or condone same-sex marriage. Sider argues that evangelicals should not have tolerated hatred and discrimination against gays and lesbians and ignored the more serious threat to marriage: heterosexual adultery and divorce. He suggests that evangelicals fight for marriage against all threats, especially the redefinition of marriage.*

Ron Sider, "Bearing Better Witness," *First Things*, December 2010. www.FirstThings.com.
Copyright © 2010 by Institute on Religion and Public Life. Reproduced by permission.

As you read, consider the following questions:

1. According to the author, what countries have charged pastors for hate crimes because they preached sermons condemning homosexual practice as sin?

2. According to Sider, what percentage of young churchgoers believe contemporary Christianity is antihomosexual?

3. As outlined by the author, what changes should evangelicals advocate in the divorce laws?

When even *Christianity Today* is asking, "Is the Gay Marriage Debate Over?" the issue has become so critical that it demands close attention. Believing (wrongly) that the debate is over, some evangelicals have decided that Christians should let the state define marriage any way it chooses and focus their attention only on what the Church does. This would be a fundamental mistake. The debate is one in which we must be involved for the sake of our society itself. Even a state such as ours, which does not use the law to promote or discourage particular religious beliefs, nevertheless has a huge stake in marriage. It is not simply a religious issue. The law is a moral teacher. Most people assume that if something is legal, it is moral—or at least not immoral. What is legal soon will become normal. Every society requires an ongoing supply of babies who grow up to be good citizens. Every civilization has known what contemporary sociologists now demonstrate: Children grow best into wholesome adults when they live with their biological mother and father. Marriage law is a crucial way in which the state promotes the sound nurturing of the next generation of citizens.

Legalizing gay marriage would weaken the connection between marriage and procreation—and the connection between biological parents and their biological children—which is why court cases in support of gay marriage typically downgrade the role of procreation. The Massachusetts Supreme Court said that the state is indifferent to family structure. When Canada legalized same-sex marriage, it tossed out the definition of "natural" parent and replaced it with "legal" parent.

## Gay Rights vs. Religious Freedom

Most legal scholars agree that if gay marriage receives the sanction of law, "gay rights" will be pitted against the rights of religious freedom—and, more often than not, will win. Gay activists will argue that government cannot "subsidize discrimination," and the courts will generally agree. Religious institutions will find that freedom to practice and even say what they believe about sexuality and marriage will increasingly be restricted. Already, in Canada and Sweden, pastors have been taken to court and charged with hate crimes because they preached sermons condemning homosexual practice as sin.

Nobody thinks churches or ministers will be forced to marry gay couples—although they may lose their legal privilege to register marriages if they refuse to do so. But through licensure and government grants a wide variety of faith-based organizations will face growing pressure to abandon their stand on homosexual practice and gay marriage.

## Consequence for Religious Organizations

There already are significant examples. More than twenty years ago, when a gay student group sued Georgetown University for refusing to grant it university recognition, the D.C. Court of Appeals concluded that "the eradication of sexual orientation discrimination outweighs any burden imposed upon Georgetown's exercise of religion." Massachusetts has required that Catholic Charities' long-established adoption program must place children with gay couples—even if the program receives no money from the commonwealth. The New York Court of Appeals ruled against Yeshiva University because it refused to permit a same-sex couple to live in its married-student housing. In San Francisco, the Salvation Army lost $3.5 million in social-service contracts because it refused, on religious grounds, to provide benefits to same-sex partners of its employees.

Faith-based organizations eventually may lose their tax-exempt status. Even the threat of such a disastrous development will move many Christian organizations to silence or change. In 1983, the Supreme Court ruled that Bob Jones University could lawfully be denied its tax exemption because of its policy on interracial dating. I vigorously agree with that decision because racism is wrong. But more and more people accept the misguided argument that opposition to homosexual practice and gay marriage is just like racism.

## A Lack of Credibility

Tragically, because of our own mistakes and sin, we evangelicals have almost no credibility on this topic. We have tolerated genuine hatred of gays; we should have taken the lead in condemning gay bashing but were largely silent; we have neglected to act in gentle love with people among us struggling with their sexual identity; and we have used the gay community as a foil to raise funds for political campaigns. We have made it easy for the media to suggest that the fanatics who carry signs announcing "God hates fags" actually speak for large numbers of evangelicals.

Worst of all, we have failed to deal honestly with the major threat to marriage and the family: heterosexual adultery and divorce. Evangelicals divorce at the same rate as the rest of the population. Many evangelical leaders have failed to speak against cheap divorce because they and their people were getting divorced just like everyone else. And yet we have had the gall to use the tiny (5 percent or less) gay community as a whipping boy that we labeled as the great threat to marriage.

What a farce. It is hardly surprising that young non-Christians' most common perception (held by 91 percent) of contemporary Christianity is that we are "antihomosexual." Even more disturbing is that 80 percent of young churchgoers agree.

We did not need to do this. We could have preached against hatred of gays, taken the lead in combating gay bashing, and been the most active community lovingly caring for people with AIDS. We could have taken marriage more seriously. We could have shown the world that Christians could defend marriage while loving those who wanted to live a different way.

## An Example of Christian Charity

The former vice president of Jerry Falwell's Liberty University, Ed Dobson, got it right. After he left Liberty to become pastor of Calvary Church in Grand Rapids, Michigan, he regularly visited a former parishioner's hospitalized son who turned out to have AIDS. Slowly, he sensed a call to serve other people with AIDS.

He decided to visit the local AIDS resource center run by the gay community. The director was shocked that the pastor of the largest evangelical church in town would visit. Dobson's church was soon deeply engaged with the gay community. Calvary placed a church member on the board of the AIDS resource center, bought Christmas gifts for families affected by AIDS, paid for funeral expenses for impoverished people who died of AIDS, and welcomed the gay community to attend the church.

Of course, it was controversial. One church member warned that the church would be "overrun by homosexuals." Dobson responded in his next Sunday sermon: "If the church gets overrun with homosexuals, that will be terrific. They can take their place in the pews right next to the liars, gossips, and materialists."

Most astonishing was an editorial that appeared in the local gay and lesbian newsletter. The writer noted that Dobson and Calvary Church believed gay sexual activity was sinful, but thanked Calvary Church for inviting gays and lesbians to their services. They knew that Dobson and his church loved them because they ministered to the people dying of AIDS.

## Setting an Example

Think of the impact if most evangelicals in the past three decades had followed Dobson's example. Then, maybe, when non-Christians heard the word "evangelical," they would think, "Oh, they are the people who love homosexuals and care for them when they are dying of AIDS." Tragically, as Dobson says, we have been better at hating than loving. As a consequence, we cannot respond effectively, with any public credibility, to the challenge to the historic understanding of marriage.

The challenge is a great one. Many Americans, including substantial numbers of evangelical youth, ask: How does granting a state marriage license to that 5 percent of the population that is gay hurt the 95 percent that is heterosexual? How can we deny the rights and privileges of marriage to gay people without violating the principles of justice, equality, and respect for individual freedom? Many Americans embrace the libertarian principle that we should maximize the freedom of each individual except where that harms others, and most believe that marriage is "primarily a way in which two adults affirm their emotional commitment to one another," as gay activist Andrew Sullivan has written.

## What Is the Definition of Marriage

If that is the proper definition of marriage, it is indeed unfair for the state to deny that privilege to a few when it grants it to the majority. But everything depends on the definition. If marriage is not about bringing up children, but about how adults solemnize their emotional commitment to each other, gay marriage becomes plausible. Other relationships become plausible as well. Why should marriage be limited to two people, for example? In fact, in 2006, prominent pro-gay activists, including Gloria Steinem and professors at Yale and Columbia, urged the state to recognize polygamous marriages and relationships of multiple sex partners.

Is emotional commitment between two adults what the state should care about in marriage? What should a state that does not establish any religion understand marriage to be? I think the answer is clear. The state must promote the best setting in which to nurture the next generation of wholesome citizens.

In a fascinating article in the *Public Interest* called "The Liberal Case Against Gay Marriage," Susan Shell argues that the state's central concern is to secure "the relation between a child and a particular set of parents." In marriage, Shell notes, "A husband is, until otherwise proven, the acknowledged father of his wife's offspring, with recognized rights and duties that may vary from society to society but always exist in some form. And a wife is a woman who can expect a certain specified sort of help from her husband in the raising of her offspring. All other functions of marriage borrow from or build upon this one."

She asks: "Can those who are not even potentially partners in reproduction, and who could never under any circumstances have been so, actually 'marry'?" Her answer is no. Whatever else one may want to say positively about the emotional commitment of two men or two women to each other, it is simply not marriage. If the central concern of the state in marriage law is to secure a good relationship between a child and its biological parents, then by definition marriage can only involve a man and a woman.

## The Best Interests of Children

Other things being equal, it is better for children to grow up with their biological parents. Marriage to the mother is by far

# Defense of Marriage Act: Definition of Marriage

In determining the meaning of any Act of Congress, or of any ruling, regulation, or interpretation of the various administrative bureaus and agencies of the United States, the word 'marriage' means only a legal union between one man and one woman as husband and wife, and the word "spouse" refers only to a person of the opposite sex who is a husband or a wife.

*H.R. 3396: Defense of Marriage Act,*
*January 3, 1996.*

the best way to ensure responsible fatherhood. When not married to the mother, few men are effective fathers. As far as the state is concerned, the first concern of marriage law must be to protect the interests of children and thereby create an ongoing, stable, wholesome social order.

It has been argued that, if the state's central interest in marriage is the raising of wholesome citizens, it should not grant a marriage license to sterile couples, those who choose not to have children, or older people who no longer can conceive children. Because the advocates of traditional marriage will not say this, the argument goes, their claims are invalid.

In fact, we do not say this because our argument actually does not imply it. The state cannot know which married men and women will be sterile. By granting couples who do not want children the status of marriage, the state recognizes that they have the kind of union that characteristically produces children, even if they choose (at first) not to have any. By granting that status to older people no longer capable of conceiving a child, the state encourages the view that sex should be limited to married persons because that strengthens the likelihood that children will be raised by their biological parents.

## Adoption and Gay Families

It also has been argued that arguments along these lines belittle adoption. My wife and I have a wonderful adopted daughter. In many situations (including abuse, neglect, and financial deprivation), adoption is much better for a child than remaining with one or both biological parents—but that does not change the fact that, other things being equal, it is better for a child to grow up with both biological parents. Even the best adoptive homes recognize that the absence of biological parents brings painful struggles.

Many gay partners argue that their home is just as good for children as that of a married man and woman. We do not have the careful, longitudinal comparative studies needed to demonstrate whether they are right or wrong, but we know that adopted children in even the best families experience emotional anguish at the loss of their biological parents, and family systems studies show that adolescents develop their own sexual identity best when they have both male and female role models. It is certainly reasonable, on the basis of what we now know, to make the claim that, other things being equal, it is better for children to grow up with both biological parents.

Some also argue that it is better for a child to be adopted by gay partners than to grow up in an orphanage or poor foster home. But even if it were, that does not warrant changing the historic definition of marriage.

## Redefining Marriage and Taking Action

The evidence, as we have seen, is clear: The legal redefinition of marriage would have far-reaching negative consequences. Abandoning what every civilization for millennia has understood marriage to be would harm children and undermine religious freedom. What can we evangelicals, who have lost almost all our credibility to speak on this topic, do to promote the historic understanding of marriage?

First, we must truly repent of the deep, widespread antigay prejudice in evangelical circles. We must ask forgiveness for our failures of love and concern and stop elevating the sin of homosexual practice above other sins.

In the life of the local church, we must distinguish homosexual orientation and practice. Someone who is publicly known to have a gay orientation but lives a celibate life should be just as eligible for church leadership as a heterosexual person who has been promiscuous but now lives in a faithful heterosexual marriage or remains celibate. We should develop church settings where celibate persons with a gay orientation can experience strong, supportive Christian community.

Second, we must set our own house in order by dramatically reducing in our families the devastation and havoc caused by heterosexual disobedience. Our argument that the tiny gay community undermines marriage is hypocritical unless we admit that by far the greatest threat to marriage and family is the sinful failure of husbands and wives to keep their marriage vows. If we cannot resist adultery and divorce and model wholesome, joyful family life, we should admit that we have nothing credible to say in the public discussion of marriage.

Almost everyone longs for something better. Jesus' followers know the answer to that longing. Evangelical husbands and wives who keep their marriage vows for a lifetime and raise their biological (and adopted) children in joyful, wholesome families would be one of our most powerful evangelistic tools. They would also give us credibility when we promote the historic understanding of marriage.

To do this we will need to teach biblical truths on sexuality, marriage, and divorce at every level, from preteens through retirees. We will need extensive Christian marriage counseling and programs such as Marriage Savers. We will need to resist the culture's narcissistic individualism, already too visible in our churches, and develop congregations that are communities of mutual accountability and even church discipline—in the wonderful words of John Wesley, "Watching over one another in love."

Third, we should seek to change the divorce laws, especially no-fault divorce. When children are involved, the law should deny no-fault divorce and in other ways make divorce more difficult. This, not gay marriage, is the area of marriage law that affects the vast majority of our children. We should be spending the overwhelming majority of the time we devote to marriage law to changing the law that permits cheap divorce for heterosexuals.

Finally, we must treat gay people fairly. Gay couples want to have, and deserve to have, such basic rights as that of the family member or spouse to visit a loved one in the hospital. One significant way to give them these rights would be to support the legal recognition of civil unions. (These unions also should be available to such others as a single person looking after an aging parent or a bachelor brother and spinster sister running a business together.)

## Push Civil Unions, Not Same-Sex Marriage

Other legal procedures might meet gay people's concerns. But I see no problem with a carefully written law that defines a number of rights as part of a legally recognized civil union. That does not mean that those rights should include everything but the name of marriage. Given the purpose of marriage law, some rights and benefits—specifically those designed to strengthen the likelihood that children grow up with both biological parents—belong only to those who are married and not to those in civil unions. That would be fair, and also a test. If the gay community's real agenda is to legitimize the homosexual lifestyle, the community will reject civil unions. If the agenda is, as many now claim, to gain appropriate benefits and rights, the gay community will accept civil unions and not press for gay marriage.

"*Section 3 of [the Defense of Marriage Act] was designed, not to promote a constitutionally legitimate federal interest, but to enforce a distinctive animus against homosexuals. And . . . Judge Tauro . . . rightly declared this congressional travesty unconstitutional.*"

# The Defense of Marriage Act Is Unconstitutional

*Geoffrey R. Stone*

*Geoffrey R. Stone is an author and the Edward H. Levi Distinguished Service Professor of Law at the University of Chicago. In the following viewpoint, he discusses the 2010 ruling by a federal judge that the Defense of Marriage Act (DOMA) violates the constitutional right of married same-sex couples to equal protection under the law and reverses the federal government's long history of allowing states to set their own marriage laws. Stone concurs with the ruling of the court that the creation of DOMA was motivated by a specific animus toward gays and lesbians—usually based in religious beliefs—and is therefore unconstitutional.*

As you read, consider the following questions:

1. Which American president appointed federal judge Joseph L. Tauro, as reported by Stone?

2. According to the author, which entities were responsible for defining what constitutes "marriage" before 1996?

3. According to Stone, does the Supreme Court recognize that government can lawfully treat one group of people worse than others because the majority deems that minority group "immoral" or sinful according to "God's principles"?

In his recent decision in *Gill v. Office of Personnel Management*, federal judge Joseph L. Tauro held unconstitutional Section 3 of the Defense of Marriage Act (DOMA). In reaching this result, Judge Tauro, who was appointed by [President] Richard Nixon, addressed a subtle but important issue of constitutional law.

The federal government provides many benefits to married couples. For example, the spouse of a federal employee is entitled to medical coverage, the spouse of an individual covered by Social Security is eligible for retirement and survivor benefits, and married couples who file joint tax returns usually pay considerably lower federal income taxes than individuals who file separately.

## A Federal Power Grab

Before 1996, all federal programs providing marriage benefits left the definition of "marriage" entirely to the states. If a couple was legally married under state law, then they were "married" for purposes of federal law. This was so even though States often have quite different rules about marriage. Some states, for example, recognize common law marriage, most do not. Some states allow people to marry without parental consent at age of 15, others require them to be at least 18. Some states permit individuals to terminate a marriage without any finding of fault, others do not. In all these circumstances, federal law defers to the state's definition of marriage. Indeed, from the very founding of our nation, the definition of marriage has been understood to be a state—rather than a federal—responsibility.

In 1996, however, Congress suddenly jettisoned this deeply rooted tradition and attempted to interpose a new federal definition of marriage. The precipitating event was a debate in Hawaii over the legal recognition of same-sex marriage. Vilifying gays as "immoral" and "depraved," and condemning same-sex marriage as "perverse" and as "an attack on God's principles," members of Congress pushed through Section 3 of DOMA, which for the first time in our nation's history adopted a federal definition of marriage, confining "marriage" for federal purposes to only those legally-recognized marriages that are "between one man and one woman."

What makes the *Gill* case so interesting is that it raises a question somewhat different from that posed by State laws that decline to recognize same-sex marriage. Because the states have primary authority over the institution of marriage, they can appropriately consider a broad range of factors in deciding who can marry, in what circumstances, and subject to what conditions. The federal government, on the other hand, has no such authority.

For example, a state can lawfully enact a law prohibiting any person under the age of 18 to marry, but for Congress to enact such a law would clearly intrude on the authority of the States. Similarly, whether or not a state can constitutionally prohibit same-sex marriage, Congress plainly has no authority to do so.

## An Intriguing Paradox

DOMA, however, does not go that far. It does not prohibit States from legalizing same-sex marriage. Rather, it refuses to defer to a State's definition of marriage, insofar as it embraces same-sex marriage, for the purpose of determining eligibility for federal benefits. DOMA therefore poses an interesting puzzle. The federal government is under no obligation to provide special benefits to married couples, but if it chooses to do so can it discriminate against some marriages and not others? This question implicates the constitutional guarantee of "equal protection of the laws."

For example, the government need not provide any health benefits to its employees, but if it chooses to do so it cannot constitutionally deny those benefits to particular employees because they are black, or women, or Mormon, or of Irish ancestry. The greater power—not to provide benefits at all—does not necessarily include the lesser power—to provide benefits only to some employees, but not others. This is at the very heart of the constitutional guarantee of equality.

Of course, differential treatment of different people is not *always* unconstitutional. If it was, then legislation would be pretty much impossible. For example, although the government cannot deny health benefits to employees because they are black or Mormon, it presumably can deny such benefits to employees who work only part-time.

## Questions of Equality

In giving meaning to the constitutional guarantee of equality, the Supreme Court has focused on three types of situations. First, a law may discriminate against a group that, like blacks and women, has historically been discriminated against on the basis of a more or less immutable characteristic. Second, a law may discriminate between individuals with respect to a fundamental interest, such as the right to vote or the right to procreate. In these first two situations, the Court generally applies a very demanding standard of justification in deciding whether the inequality is constitutional.

In *Gill,* the court might have invoked either or both of these arguments, for sexual orientation is arguably analogous to race and gender, and marriage is arguably a fundamental interest. Judge Tauro, however, found it unnecessary to address those questions.

Instead, he analyzed DOMA as if it fell into the third situation, which consists of laws that neither implicate a fundamental interest nor discriminate against a group that is analogous to blacks and women. In this third situation, the Supreme Court generally finds a law constitutional if it rationally furthers a legitimate government interest. This would be the case, for example, if the government denied health benefits to part-time employees.

In *Gill,* Judge Tauro held that DOMA's discrimination against legally-married same-sex couples failed to satisfy even this more deferential standard. In enacting Section 3, members of Congress argued that the denial of equal benefits to same-sex couples who are legally married under state law encourages "responsible procreation," promotes "heterosexual marriage," and preserves "morality." But whatever one thinks of these interests when offered in defense of a State's decision not to recognize same-sex marriage, they carry much less weight when advanced by Congress to justify discrimination against couples who are already legally-married. And this is especially true in a realm in which Congress traditionally has no business meddling in the first place.

## Rejecting Blatant Discrimination

Moreover, the Supreme Court has long recognized that the government can never lawfully treat one group of people worse than others because the majority deems that group "immoral," "depraved," unworthy, or sinful according to "God's principles." Such animus is not a constitutionally legitimate basis for government action. Yet this seems to be precisely what motivated Section 3 of DOMA.

Indeed, if we acknowledge, as we must, that Congress had never before second-guessed a state's definition of marriage, and that the interests said to justify Section 3 have traditionally been understood to be within the exclusive domain of the States, it is difficult not to wonder what was really going on in Congress when it enacted DOMA.

After all, if Congress was truly serious about its purported justifications for DOMA, then it would have re-defined "marriage" to exclude other "depraved" or "immoral" unions. For example, it might have held that convicted mass murderers, child molesters, rapists, and adulterers cannot "marry" for purposes of receiving marriage benefits under federal law. But Congress apparently saw no reason to second-guess the states in their decisions to allow such persons to marry. It was *only* on the issue of sexual orientation that Congress saw fit to intervene.

In such circumstances, it is hard not to conclude that Section 3 of DOMA was designed, not to promote a constitutionally legitimate federal interest, but to enforce a distinctive animus against homosexuals. And it was precisely for this reason that Judge Tauro, following two major Supreme Court precedents invalidating other laws that discriminated on the basis of sexual orientation, rightly declared this congressional travesty unconstitutional.

# Periodical and Internet Sources Bibliography

*The following articles have been selected to supplement the diverse views presented in this chapter.*

| | |
|---|---|
| Daniel Burke | "Another 8 Debate: Should Religious Views Factor into Voting?" *Washington Post*, August 14, 2010. |
| CNN.com | "Congress Debates Biblical Stance on Immigration," July 14, 2010. |
| Chuck Colson | "Freedom of Religion at Stake," *Christian Post*, July 7, 2010. |
| William Douglas | "Immigration Debate Turns to Religion," *Charlotte (NC) Observer*, July 15, 2010. |
| Jonah Goldberg | "An Ugly Attack on Mormons," *Los Angeles Times*, December 2, 2008. |
| Robert P. Jones and Daniel Cox | "The Surprising Religious Divides on Proposition 8," CNN.com, August 5, 2010. |
| Jamilah Lemieux | "Why Prop 8 and 9/11 Mosque Matter to Us," *Essence*, August 18, 2010. |
| Thomas Messner | "Religion and Morality in the Same-Sex Marriage Debate," The Heritage Foundation *Backgrounder* no. 2437, July 20, 2010. |
| Irene Monroe | "Race, Religion, and Proposition 8," *Advocate*, November 12, 2008. |
| James Murr | "Religion and Politics Really Don't Mix," *Santa Maria (CA) Times*, September 17, 2010. |
| Harris R. Sherline | "California's Proposition 8 Revisited," GOPUSA.com, October 11, 2010. |
| Geoffrey R. Stone | "Democracy, Religion and Proposition 8," HuffingtonPost.com, November 15, 2008. |

OPPOSING
VIEWPOINTS®
SERIES

# CHAPTER 4

# How Does the Separation of Church and State Affect Other Issues?

# Chapter Preface

The "Don't Ask, Don't Tell' (DADT) policy has been a hot potato with American politicians since it went into effect in 1993 under President Bill Clinton. DADT was essentially a compromise: Clinton had made a campaign promise that he would work to pass legislation that would allow gays and lesbians to serve in the military openly; Congress overrode Clinton, citing Department of Defense directives that stated that homosexuality was incompatible with military service. So the Clinton administration came up with an unwieldy compromise: military applicants could not be asked about their sexual orientation, and gay soldiers and sailors could not reveal their homosexuality; hence, Don't Ask, Don't Tell.

However, it quickly became apparent that DADT was a problematic policy. Under the policy, gays and lesbians were not allowed to serve openly and were forced to hide their sexual orientation from superiors and even colleagues. If a gay soldier's sexual orientation became known, he or she could be discharged. In fact, since the policy was implemented in 1993, approximately fourteen thousand servicemen and servicewomen have been discharged under DADT.

During his 2008 presidential campaign, Barack Obama campaigned for the repeal of the DADT policy. Studies released in 2010 showed that the military was ready for such a move. The Pentagon's Comprehensive Review Working Group report concluded that "the risk of repeal of don't ask, don't tell to overall military effectiveness is low." US secretary of defense Robert Gates and the chairman of the Joint Chiefs of Staff, Admiral Mike Mullen, both told the Senate Armed Services Committee on December 2, 2010, that DADT repeal should happen in 2010–2011.

In some quarters there was still significant opposition to the repeal of DADT. Some of the strongest objections came from military chaplains, who believed they would be forced to compromise their religious belief that homosexuality is a sin and that same-sex relationships and unions are immoral. As Archbishop for the Military USA Timothy Broglio stated,

> There is no doubt that morality and the corresponding good moral decisions have an effect on unit cohesion and the overall morale of the troops and effectiveness of the mission. This Archdiocese exists to serve those who serve and it assists them by advocating moral behavior. The military must find ways to promote that behavior and develop strong prohibitions against any immoral activity that would jeopardize morale, good morals, unit cohesion and every other factor that weakens the mission. So also must a firm effort be made to avoid any injustices that may inadvertently develop because individuals or groups are put in living situations that are an affront to good common sense.

Supporters of the DADT repeal argued that no military chaplain would be required to change his or her beliefs or remain silent on the church's position on homosexuality. Furthermore, no chaplain would be required to perform a same-sex marriage or bless a same-sex union. They point out that the military is a secular institution, which has the right to include whomever it deems acceptable. It is not the church's role to determine who can serve and who cannot.

Ultimately, the opposition to DADT repeal was overcome. On December 18, 2010, the Senate voted to end debate on S.4023, the bill to repeal the DADT policy. Senator Joe Lieberman gave the final argument in favor of repealing DADT, and Senator John McCain argued against repeal. The final Senate vote was held later that day, and the measure passed by a vote of 65–31. Following the vote, Secretary Gates announced an immediate plan for implementation as soon as conditions are met for an orderly repeal. President Obama signed the repeal into law on December 22, 2010.

The debate over the role of religion in the DADT repeal is one of the topics examined in the following chapter, which focuses on how the principle of church-state separation influences a number of controversial issues in the United States. Other topics include the Cordoba House, also known as the Ground Zero mosque; teaching intelligent design in school; and removing the words "under God" from the Pledge of Allegiance.

| *"Religion should not be imposed on public spaces."*

# Banning the Cordoba House Would Be a Violation of the Separation of Church and State

*Katha Pollitt*

*Katha Pollitt is an author, political columnist, and a fellow at the Nation Institute. In the following viewpoint, she reminds readers that the First Amendment of the US Constitution protects the freedom of speech and religion of all Americans, including the Muslim group that wants to build a community center two blocks away from the site of the September 11, 2001, terrorist attacks. Pollitt believes the opposition to the project is rooted in religious intolerance, and finds it unacceptable in a country where religious tolerance is the law.*

As you read, consider the following questions:

1. According to the author, how much money is the Cordoba House estimated to cost?

2. What does Pollitt make of Newt Gingrich's argument that the United States cannot let Muslims build a mosque at Ground Zero because Saudi Arabia does not permit the building of churches and synagogues?

3. How many billion Muslims are there worldwide, according to the author?

Park51, *aka* [also known as] Cordoba House, won't be a mosque; it will be a $100 million, thirteen-story cultural center with a pool, gym, auditorium and prayer room. It won't be at Ground Zero; it will be two blocks away. (By the way, two mosques have existed in the neighborhood for years.) It won't be a shadowy storefront where radical clerics recruit young suicide bombers; it will be a showplace of moderate Islam, an Islam for the pluralist West—the very thing wise heads in the United States and Europe agree is essential to integrate Muslim immigrants and prevent them from becoming fundamentalists and even terrorists. "It's a shame we even have to talk about this," says Mayor Michael Bloomberg, a longtime supporter of the project.

## Ignoring the First Amendment

Apparently we do, because the same right-wingers who talk about the Constitution as if Sarah Palin had tweeted it herself apparently skipped over the First Amendment, where freedom of speech and worship are guaranteed to all. "America is experiencing an Islamist cultural-political offensive designed to undermine and destroy our civilization," claims Newt Gingrich, who argues that the United States can't let Muslims build a "mosque" "at Ground Zero" because Saudi Arabia doesn't permit the building of churches and synagogues. For a man who warns that Sharia law is coming soon to a courthouse near you, Gingrich seems strangely eager to accept Saudi standards of religious tolerance. Isn't the whole point that ours is an open society and theirs is closed? "This is a desecration," says former Mayor Rudy Giuliani. "Nobody would allow something like that at Pearl Harbor. Let's have some respect for who died there and why they died there. Let's not put this off on some kind of politically correct theory." I'm not aware of any Japanese-Americans trying to build a Shinto shrine at Pearl Harbor, but what if they had? Why would that be so terrible? (Oh, and "politically correct theory"? Would that be the First Amendment? Giuliani never did have much fondness for pesky old free speech.)

And then there's Sarah Palin, America's Tweetheart: "Peace-seeking Muslims, pls understand, Ground Zero mosque is UNNECESSARY provocation; it stabs hearts. Pls reject it in interest of healing." Yes, peace-seeking Muslims, just crawl back into your cave and leave us real Americans alone so we can get over the terrible crime committed by people who are not you! Thirty-three years ago, the language of healing wasn't powerful enough to keep the National Socialists of America from marching in Skokie, Illinois—home to many Holocaust survivors—and kudos to the ACLU [American Civil Liberties Union] for defending the freedom of assembly even of those worst of the worst, a position that was not at all obvious at the time. But we've been thoroughly bathed in psychobabble since then, so it's not surprising that sophisticated opponents like Abraham Foxman, national director of the Anti-Defamation League, have adopted that cloying lingo: "strong passions . . . keen sensitivities . . . counterproductive to the healing process." As Foxman wrote in a statement, "ultimately this is not a question of rights, but a question of what is right. In our judgment, building an Islamic Center in the shadow of the World Trade Center will cause some victims more pain—unnecessarily—and that is not right."

## Religious Tolerance Must Prevail

Actually, there are 9/11 survivors and families on both sides of the Park51 proposal. Opening the center is "consistent with

# What Is the Cordoba House/Park51?

Park51 will grow into a world-class community center, planned to include the following facilities:

- outstanding recreation spaces and fitness facilities (swimming pool, gym, basketball court)

- 500-seat auditorium

- a restaurant and culinary school

- cultural amenities including exhibitions

- education programs

- a library, reading room and art studios

- childcare services

- a prayer space, intended to be run separately from Park51 but open to and accessible to all members, visitors and our New York community

- a September 11th memorial and quiet contemplation space, open to all

*Park51 website. www.blog.park51.org.*

fundamental American values of freedom and justice for all," said the group September 11 Families for Peaceful Tomorrows. And although a Marist poll found that 53 percent of New York City residents oppose the center, 53 percent of Manhattanites support it—let's hear it for the much-mocked Upper West Side. But even if all the survivors, and every inhabitant of the World Trade Center's home borough, were united against it, that should not carry the day. The Constitution is not a Tylenol pill. It's not about making hurt people feel better—or pandering to the resentments of bigots, either. Nor is it about polls or majority votes. If it were, freedom of speech would not be possible, because as [political theorist] Rosa Luxemburg said, freedom is "always . . . for the one who thinks differently." It would be nice if our elected officials, who swore an oath to defend the Constitution, got the message. Instead, we have mostly silence, with Governor David Paterson offering state land if Park51 agreed to move elsewhere. That man just can't seem to do anything right.

What's especially odd about the Park51 flap is that Palin, Gingrich and other right-wing opponents delight in waving the Constitution about and professing to revere its every word. They, after all, are the ones who love religion so much, they think the First Amendment is all about privileging it over secularism. Don't tread on me with your evil humanist jackboot! The argument that religion should not be imposed on public spaces—a public-school classroom, say—has never made sense to them. In their mythology, believers are a persecuted minority because the ACLU won't let biology teachers suggest that Earth might well be only 10,000 years old. It turns out that by religion they mean only Christianity. Indeed, Tennessee Tea Party gubernatorial candidate Ron Ramsey suggests that Islam isn't a religion but a cult—as if the world's 1.5 billion Muslims are sleep-deprived runaways controlled by an evil mastermind.

The attempt by Gingrich and others to portray Park51 as part of a planned Islamic takeover of the United States is shameful and ridiculous. America is a secular democracy in which at least three-quarters of the population are committed Christians, and hedonism is a way of life. Almost nobody, even among American Muslims, is interested in the supposed aims of militant Islam—polygyny, forcing women into burqas, banning pork and alcohol and music, instituting Sharia law. Fear of Muslim rule is even more preposterous than what it has so efficiently replaced—fear of communist rule—and one day it will look just as bizarre.

By then, I hope Park51 will be a modern landmark in the city Mayor Bloomberg proudly called the freest in the world.

*"It is the very First Amendment that . . . permits New Yorkers to block the construction of a mosque."*

# Banning the Cordoba House Would Not Be a Violation of the Separation of Church and State

*George Neumayr*

*George Neumayr is editor of* Catholic World Report *and is a press critic for the* California Political Review. *In the following viewpoint, he contends that it is not a violation of church-state separation to ban the Cordoba House—a proposed Muslim community center to be built in New York two blocks from the site of the September 11, 2001, terrorist attacks—because the First Amendment was drafted by the nation's Founding Fathers to protect the majority from a religious minority. Neumayr accuses the Barack Obama administration of favoring Muslims over the Christian majority in America and of being willfully ignorant of the threat Islam and the Cordoba House pose to the country.*

As you read, consider the following questions:

1. What actions does the author cite as evidence that the Obama administration favors Islam?

2. What did Tunisian envoy Sidi Soliman Mellimelli request from Secretary of State James Madison, according to Neumayr?

3. According to the author, why did Thomas Jefferson own a Koran?

By modern secularist standards, [President] Barack Obama's boosterism for Islam violates the "separation between Church and state." Had [President] George W. Bush held a rosary and modest fish dinner at the White House to mark the beginning of Lent, the ACLU [American Civil Liberties Union] left would have freaked out. But these same secularists didn't mind Barack's "Iftar dinner" [celebrating the breaking of the Muslim Ramadan fast] last Friday night.

That is, until he wimped out on his endorsement of the Ground Zero mosque. Now his dinner looks to them more like the production of *Ishtar* [an infamously bad big-budget movie of 1987], as finger-to-the-wind Dems cravenly scramble for cover. The search is on for a "compromise." Perhaps the self-styled Solomonic Obama can convince the mosque planners to transfer their property rights to NASA. Administrator Charles Bolden could then turn the land into a satellite office for contractors who pursue the space agency's "perhaps foremost" mission (as explained to him by Obama): "to reach out to the Muslim world and engage much more with dominantly Muslim nations to help them feel good about their historic contribution to science . . . and math and engineering."

## Pandering to Muslims

The moment one thinks this presidency has hit the bottom of grim parody it finds a new one. It is hard to keep track of them at this point, but any list of the White House's greatest Islamophilic hits would have to include: wanting a civilian jury trial for the 9/11 planners, refusing to identify radical Islam as a terrorist motive, endorsing the concept of jihad, fretting over the loss of "diversity" after the Fort Hood shooting, and vacationing through the fallout of an aborted Christmas day bombing over Detroit.

The White House's ideologically willful self-delusion about radical Islam is staggering. Here, for example, is its self-reporting at whitehouse.gov about the Ramadan dinner: "Last night, President Obama continued the White House tradition of hosting an Iftar—the meal that breaks the day of fasting—celebrating Ramadan in the State Dining Room." Continued a tradition? Exactly which White House tradition is that?

The answer: Obama was referring not to a White House "tradition" but to one distant event that he carefully left vague: Thomas Jefferson's war negotiations with Tunisian envoy Sidi Soliman Mellimelli.

## Jefferson and Islam

Jefferson, desperate to end the Barbary war with Islamic pirates, invited Mellimelli to Washington for negotiations. According to Gave Wilson, the visit put Jefferson and his staff on the spot: James Madison, then the Secretary of State, had to field Mellimelli's request for "concubines." Jefferson told shocked colleagues to calm down; after all, peace with the Barbary pirates required passing "unnoticed the irregular conduct of their ministers." Mellimelli, in his own way, was grateful. After hearing some gossip about the wan mood of the childless Madisons, he "flung his 'magical' cloak around Dolley Madison and murmured an incantation that promised she would bear a male child. His conjuring, however, did not work."

The war negotiations happened to coincide with Ramadan. Consequently, a scheduled dinner at the White House had to

## The Ground Zero Mosque Controversy

Nationally, the fight over the [Ground Zero] mosque has escalated far beyond name-calling into an emotional, politically driven war over American values. Does being American mean holding the personal pain of some above the constitutional rights of others, as the Anti-Defamation League suggested in its statement proposing the mosque move somewhere else? Or does it mean seeing this country as a mighty power with a God-given mission to right global wrongs—rhetoric not heard since George W. Bush and the "Axis of Evil" days? Republicans running for election have seized on the mosque and Imam Rauf as symbols of what they see as President Obama's inadequate and politically correct response to the terrorist threat.

*Lisa Miller, Newsweek, August 8, 2010.*

be moved back from "half after three" to "precisely at sunset" in order for Mellimelli to show up.

While it is true that the basically agnostic Jefferson was an arrogant secularist in embryo (the type on display now who dislikes all religions save Islam), he was under no illusions about jihadists. The Obama White House makes references to the "Koran" Jefferson owned, as if he had purchased it for religious edification. The truth is that he purchased it for self-protection: he wanted to understand the attitudes and war tactics of the Barbary pirates.

## Misinterpreting the Constitution

The cocky frat-boy "Republican" on *MSNBC*, Joe Scarborough, a hopelessly smug lightweight who tries to weigh in on the "big issues" of the day when not playing early-morning grabass with his equally shallow but self-important guests, has said repeatedly that the Founding Fathers wrote the First Amendment to protect projects like the Ground Zero mosque. No, they didn't. "Morning Joe" is mistaking Thurgood Marshall's "living" Constitution for theirs.

While the Founding Fathers certainly didn't want anyone coerced in matters of faith, they wrote it to protect the states from a future federal government that might swoop down and crush the public religious life of majorities in those states. (And, by the way, let's cut the PC [politically correct] crap about Jefferson as the father of the First Amendment; he wasn't even at the Constitutional Convention. He was in France as an ambassador, gazing with approval at budding French Revolutionaries.) For many decades after the Constitution was enacted several states still had religious litmus tests for public office and sent tax dollars directly to the churches of their choice.

In other words, it is the very First Amendment that Scarborough mangles which permits New Yorkers to block the construction of a mosque. The First Amendment was designed to protect the majority from the tyranny of a religious minority favored by the federal government. What radical Islam's useful idiots in the White House and the press call "religious freedom," the founders would have called insanely dumb religious relativism and self-hating stupidity.

> *"The separation of church and state is not threatened by a change in the DADT policy."*

# Repealing the "Don't Ask, Don't Tell" Policy Maintains the Separation of Church and State

*Gene Robinson*

*Gene Robinson is the ninth bishop of the Diocese of New Hampshire in the Episcopal Church and the church's first openly gay bishop; he is also a senior fellow at the Center for American Progress. In the following viewpoint, he supports the right of military chaplains to follow their religious beliefs as they pertain to homosexuality, but points out that their religious beliefs have nothing to do with allowing gays and lesbians to serve openly in the military. Robinson maintains that religious groups do not have the right to impose their religious beliefs on the secular state and its military.*

Gene Robinson, "Yes, We Do Need Separation of Church and State," AmericanProgress .org, June 10, 2010. Copyright © 2010 by Center for American Progress. Reproduced by permission.

As you read, consider the following questions:

1. What did Archbishop for the Military Services USA Timothy Broglio say in a statement released in June 2010, as cited by the author?

2. How does Broglio compare homosexuals to alcoholics in his June 2010 statement, according to Robinson?

3. How does the author refute the comparison of homosexuals to alcoholics?

Archbishop for the Military Services USA Timothy Broglio released a statement earlier this month arguing that the federal government should not repeal the military's "Don't Ask, Don't Tell" policy, which prevents gay and lesbian men and women from serving openly in the military. He claims that doing so would compromise the faith and role of Roman Catholic military chaplains. In reality, nothing could be further from the truth. His arguments are so spurious and misguided it is hard to find a place to begin in refuting them.

The separation of church and state is not threatened by a change in the DADT policy, despite the archbishop's claims. No Roman Catholic chaplain, nor any other chaplain with negative views of homosexuality, will be required to teach, preach, or counsel anything outside their own beliefs. No gay or lesbian serving in the military would expect to go to such a chaplain and receive a blessing on his or her sexual orientation.

The archbishop restates in his letter what everyone knows: The Roman Catholic Church believes and teaches that "homosexual acts are intrinsically disordered" and "are contrary to the natural law" and that "Homosexual persons are called to chastity." If you go to a chaplain with those beliefs under a repealed DADT, that's still what you're going to get in the way of counsel. What you *won't* get under the repeal is a dishonorable discharge to boot!

# Top 10 Reasons to Repeal "Don't Ask, Don't Tell" (DADT)

1. END DISCRIMINATION. No other law mandates firing someone because they are lesbian, gay or bisexual.

2. STRENGTHEN MILITARY READINESS. . . . [DADT] has resulted in the discharge of over 11,000 service members. . . .

3. SAVE TAX PAYER MONEY. A 2006 Blue Ribbon Commission report found that [DADT] caused the Pentagon to waste over $360 million in tax payer funds between 1994 and 2003.

4. HONOR OUR TROOPS. The at least 65,000 lesbian, gay, and bisexual Americans currently serving in the US Armed Forces, and one million gay veterans, should not be treated as second class citizens.

5. STOP THE DOUBLE-STANDARD. [DADT] requires gay service members to hide the truth about who they are. . . .

6. STAND UP FOR WOMEN. . . . [women] account for 30% of discharges under [DADT].

7. JOIN OUR ALLIES. American troops serve without incident side-by-side with personnel in foreign militaries and national security agencies which do not discriminate based on sexual orientation.

8. REPEAL THE HYPOCRISY. . . . discharges have dropped about 50% since 9/11.

9. LISTEN TO THE EVIDENCE. Every report commissioned by the Federal government has concluded that the ban could be lifted without determent to readiness.

10. DO WHAT'S RIGHT. Recent polls show about three-quarters of the American public believes that lesbians, gays, and bisexuals should be able to serve openly.

*"Top 10 Reasons to Repeal 'Don't Ask, Don't Tell,'" SLDN.org, 2010. Copyright © 2010 Servicemembers Legal Defense Network. Reproduced by permission.*

I wholeheartedly agree with the archbishop that "no restrictions or limitations on the teaching of Catholic morality can be accepted. First Amendment rights regarding the free exercise of religion must be respected." I would fight to the death for those protections. Fortunately, no such restrictions or limitations would be required after DADT is repealed. Period. To suggest otherwise indicates either ignorance of the proposed legislation or a disingenuousness that is not befitting a clergyman.

The archbishop goes on to say that "unions between individuals of the same gender resembling marriage will not be accepted or blessed by Catholic chaplains." Of course not. No chaplain is required to marry or bless *any* relationship against his or her will—just as no such requirement is made of any clergyperson in American society. This is a red herring—a strenuous objection to a problem that does not exist. DADT is not about relationships or marriage. It is about who is allowed to serve their country in the military.

The archbishop inexplicably goes on to drag alcoholics into the debate: "For years, those struggling with alcoholism have benefitted [sic] from Alcoholics Anonymous. Like homosexuality, there is rarely a cure. There is a control through a process, which is guarded by absolute secrecy. It is an equivalent to 'Don't ask don't tell'. The process has worked well for some time without the charge that it is discriminatory."

I can say as a recovering alcoholic *and* a gay man that there is no end to the problems with this analogy. No one would argue with the reality of the havoc created by an addiction to alcohol—a toll of pain and trouble visited on the individual, families, and society alike. No such social toll is caused by men and women proudly saying to the world, "I'm gay." Saying that there is no cure for homosexuality, as for alcoholism, is to say that there is something that *needs* curing. The archbishop is welcome to his opinion, but he must admit that it flies in the face of contrary judgments by every reputable psychiatric association in the world.

The secrecy referred to in AA is an internal protection, providing a safe place to talk about one's drinking. There is no secrecy recommended or required about being an alcoholic—only a secrecy about the identity of those one has met at an AA meeting. In fact, part of the healing process for alcoholics in AA is "coming out" to family and friends about their alcoholism, making restitution for the pain caused others, and a healthy admission of the truth: "Hello. My name is Gene, and I'm an alcoholic."

It is terribly misguided to equate Alcoholics Anonymous—which encourages its adherents to admit that they have no control over their drinking, except by the grace of a higher power—to the sheer, white-knuckled suppression of innate feelings by those who find themselves affectionally oriented to persons of the same gender. And it does justice to neither. Such a suppression of feelings is certainly possible—gay and lesbian people have been doing it for centuries, with enormous and tragic consequences. The question is: Is it right? Is it healthy? Is it what God wants for one of his beloved children? I think not.

I am not saying that the archbishop has no right to his religiously held beliefs. My question is whether the church has the right to impose those beliefs on the state. Separation of church and state works both ways! Just as the archbishop argues that he should not be coerced by the state to change his beliefs (I totally agree!), so must the church not impose its beliefs on the secular state and its military. The church has no right to argue for less-than-equal rights for any American citizen.

> "Chaplains who oppose the normaliza-
> tion of homosexual behavior in the
> military will likely face direct orders
> . . . and subtle pressure to keep their
> opposition silent."

# Repealing the "Don't Ask, Don't Tell" Policy Will Infringe on Religious Beliefs of Military Chaplains

*Daniel Blomberg*

*Daniel Blomberg serves as litigation counsel for the Alliance De-*
*fense Fund. In the following viewpoint, he contends that repeal-*
*ing the "Don't Ask Don't Tell" Policy (DADT) will severely harm*
*the ability of military chaplains to do their job, including their*
*right to preach, counsel, or teach according to their religious be-*
*liefs that homosexuality is a sin. Blomberg argues that lifting the*
*DADT ban poses a real threat to religious liberty. Congress did*
*later vote to repeal the DADT policy in December 2010.*

Daniel Blomberg, "If Gays Serve Openly, Will Chaplains Suffer? Yes, Religious Liberty Is in Real Jeopardy," USAtoday.com, July 14, 2010. Copyright © 2010 by *USA Today*. Reproduced by permission.

As you read, consider the following questions:

1. According to the author, how many high-ranking veteran chaplains signed a letter to the president complaining about repealing DADT?

2. What happened in the 2002 case of prison chaplain William Akridge, as Blomberg tells it?

3. How many religious groups have raised concerns about the repeal of DADT, according to the author?

Efforts to abolish the "don't ask, don't tell" [DADT] policy and instead allow open homosexual behavior in the military have left the U.S. armed forces in a strange state of limbo.

One of the most obvious disruptions on the horizon: the uncertain impact to the chaplaincy and the increasing concern about the effect on religious liberty if the policy is dismantled. More than 40 high-ranking and distinguished veteran chaplains signed a letter to the president and senior military officials in April [2010] outlining how the suggested changes would likely harm the ability of the chaplaincy to do its job. This harm includes limitations on the right of chaplains to preach, counsel, or teach according to their faith when doing so requires identifying homosexual behavior as sinful or detrimental.

The harm also includes restrictions on the ability of chaplains to freely conduct religious services without being forced to allow people who engage in homosexual behavior to take positions of leadership or receive sacraments, for example. And it would include forcing chaplain-administered programs, such as the Army's "Strong Bonds" marriage-building program, to modify their teaching if same-sex couples participate. Chaplains are committed to ministering to everyone but cannot allow the government to dictate how religious ministry takes place.

These concerns are not mere speculation but are based in both the practical realities of everyday chaplaincy life and numerous precedents showing that the danger to religious liberty is real.

## Cause for Concern

In the late 1990s, for instance, the [President Bill] Clinton administration tried to silence military chaplains from speaking out against "partial-birth" abortion, even banning speech in the pulpit. Similarly, chaplains who oppose the normalization of homosexual behavior in the military will likely face direct orders—potentially in the form of non-discrimination laws—and subtle pressure to keep their opposition silent, while chaplains who support the change will be free from such limitations.

Another case particularly illustrates the effect on the chaplaincy. In 2002, prison chaplain William Akridge was punished by Ohio prison officials for denying an inmate the privilege to lead chapel worship services because he actively participated in homosexual behavior. Federal courts later denied Akridge's argument that the First Amendment should give him the freedom to hold religious services according to the dictates of his faith.

If that could happen in a prison in Ohio, what should we expect in a politicized military?

An increasing number of religious bodies—including organizations that directly supply the military's chaplains—have been raising this concern. These groups include the Southern Baptist Convention, the Roman Catholic Church and more than 800 Orthodox Jewish rabbis. In addition, Professor John Martin at the Army War College has identified the religious liberty concern as one of several "significant issues" raised by the tearing down of the military's existing policy.

## Military Chaplains Urge Obama to Keep "Don't Ask Don't Tell"

We believe that normalizing homosexual conduct in the armed forces will pose a significant threat to chaplains' and service members' religious liberty. The best way to protect religious liberty—and avoid lowering widely respected religious belief to the level of racism—is simply retaining the current policy to prevent open homosexual behavior in the armed forces. At the very least, though, Congress should include comprehensive and robust religious liberty protections in any sort of policy change. Either way, we urge you to protect religious liberty, the first and foremost of America's fundamental freedoms.

*Letter to President Barack Obama, April 28, 2010.*

## Quieting Dissent

Already, constitutional rights are taking a beating. When Lt. Gen. Benjamin Mixon recommended that servicemembers speak out to Congress regarding the dismantling of "don't ask, don't tell," he was swiftly rebuked by Adm. Michael Mullen, chairman of the Joint Chiefs of Staff. Unsurprisingly, some active-duty chaplains are mum against this censorial backdrop. Why risk such censure?

Even lawmakers on Capitol Hill have dismissed the concerns of the chiefs of the Army, Air Force, Navy and Marines, who pleaded that any changes wait until a comprehensive review is completed so that we can ensure that our military's ability to fight and win wars—its primary duty—is not undermined. Congress has refused to even consider adopting statutory language that would provide some protection for religious liberty. At best, then, Congress is risking the rights of our servicemembers. At worse, they're sacrificing them for a partisan political agenda.

These political efforts have already disrupted the military mission by placing the military in a state of limbo. They should not also destroy the free religious exercise rights of those who fight and die to protect our own right to worship.

> "The 'under God' clause constitutes a
> form of prayer [and] ... is a coerced
> endorsement of religion."

# The Phrase "Under God" in the Pledge of Allegiance Is an Establishment of Religion

*Mike Whitney*

*Mike Whitney is a contributor to several periodicals. In the following viewpoint, he asserts that the phrase "under God" in the Pledge of Allegiance is unconstitutional because it is a way to force the religious beliefs of the majority on the minority. Whitney argues that Americans should stop linking expressions of patriotism with God and should, in fact, get rid of the pledge because it is incompatible with American ideals of individual liberty.*

As you read, consider the following questions:

1. Who is Michael Newdow, as introduced by the author?

2. According to Whitney, what percentage of Americans in 2000 stated that they would support an atheist political candidate?

3. According to the author, what percentage of Americans believe that we should keep the "under God" phrase in the pledge?

Michael Newdow deserves credit for persevering in his crusade to have the "under God" clause removed from the Pledge of Allegiance. [He initiated a lawsuit in 2000 on behalf of his school-age daughter against the inclusion of the phrase "under God" in the Pledge of Allegiance.] But there's a larger question to answer before he continues.

Why bother?

America is securely ensconced in religion's withering grip and Newdow's case does nothing to loosen it.

It's difficult to imagine that someone as bright as Newdow hasn't noticed the "fundamentalist" tsunami sweeping the country under the stewardship of our current President, St George of Crawford [George W. Bush]. Even the apocryphal war on terror is couched in religious rhetoric, a surefire prescription for unlimited carnage.

It's foolish to suppose that logic or science will ever crease the stony wall of conviction enclosing America's zealots. Newdow's efforts are doomed to failure. [Editor's Note: On March 11, 2010, the US Court of Appeals for the Ninth Circuit upheld the use of the words "under God" in the Pledge of Allegiance in the case of *Newdow v. Rio Linda Union School District*.]

## The Problem with the Phrase "Under God"

Yes, the "under God" clause constitutes a form of prayer.

Yes, it is a coerced endorsement of religion.

Yes, it is a way of the majority forcing their dubious beliefs on the minority.

Yes, it is an insult to anyone who either doesn't believe in God or who really hasn't made up their mind.

And, yes, Newdow's daughter is being asked to participate in a ritual that says "her father is wrong" (his atheistic beliefs) every day.

But what is Newdow expecting?

Is he expecting a wave of reason and common sense to flood the nation?

Or is he just "tilting at windmills" for his 15 minutes of fame?

## The Position of Atheists and Agnostics

Atheists and agnostics have an unusual place in American society. The discrimination is not flagrant, but it is quite real all the same. In the 1960s, the polls indicated that less than 30% of the public would vote for Jews, Blacks or atheists. In 2000 nearly 80% of the people polled said they would support either a black or Jewish candidate. Regrettably, the percentages for atheists dithered in the 25% range, indicating the widespread distrust in those who challenge the notion of a Supreme Being.

These numbers demonstrate that belief in God is still considered a fundamental requirement of good citizenships.

## Historical Revisionism

It is understandable, then, given the rise in fundamentalism, and the unalloyed fervor that issues from the White House, that the nation's founders would be recast as latter day saints rather than [as] pillars of The Enlightenment. In fact, none of the founders (Jefferson, Adams, Paine, Franklin etc.) accepted the divinity of Christ. (Jefferson's Bible scrupulously removed all of the "alleged" miracles Christ performed, thinking that they were more illustrative of a charlatan than a saint.) This seems to escape the attention of today's religious enthusiasts. The founders have been refashioned in the image of John Brown, Bible-wielding soothsayer, rather than John Locke, architect of modern democracy.

This curious bit of revisionism has led many to believe that the Constitution is the progeny of the Ten Commandments rather than the French Revolution. The strong emphasis on liberty, equality and secular government has suddenly morphed into a belief that the state should be the agent for carrying out God's Law. This is due in large part to the Bush steering committee aligning itself with fanatics like [televangelists] Franklin Graham and Pat Robertson, and appointing men like John "the Baptist" Ashcroft and General William Boykin to high office.

## Movement Toward Religious Fanaticism

Spearheaded by a President who is certain of his Messianic role in history, America is tipping towards "bin Ladenism;" a fanatical attachment to superstition as the organizing principle of society. President Bush would be more comfortable exhorting the masses in a revival tent than from the halls of Congress. His Manichean [dualistic] world view and his penchant for religious jargon have spawned a crusading mentality that is incompatible with secular government. Never the less, he has emboldened those who would like to see an even greater merging of church and state. Keeping the "under God" clause in the Pledge only strengthens their resolve.

87% of Americans believe that we should keep the "under God" clause in the Pledge.

Similarly, 87% (according to [2004] polls) of Americans profess to believe in a supreme being. This is hardly a coincidence. It points out the grim fact that people "of faith" invariably attempt to include others within their net of belief.

No, thank you.

## The Pledge as a Loyalty Oath

Religious people are the same in one regard. Their deepest, most heartfelt convictions are grounded in pure ether. Their world view is not shaped by concrete realities, but through attachment to unproved assumptions and conjecture. This is why the "under God" clause is of such great importance to them. It is a way of coercing those with other perspectives to endorse their dubious point of view.

Consensus is the baling wire that keeps the rogue elements in line with the faithful.

The "under God" debate is reducible to one brief question, "Who knows?" (Whether God exists)

We should honor that mystery and stop linking expressions of patriotism with belief in God.

The real failing of Newdow's case is not its extremism, but its timidity. The Pledge of Allegiance is an abomination from the get-go. Democracies should not require "loyalty oaths" and that's precisely what the pledge is. Our children should not be encouraged to profess their loyalty to the state; that's the behavior we expect in tyrannies. Let the representatives of the state (politicians and public servants) profess their commitment to "We the People."

## Get Rid of the Pledge

The whole idea of the pledge is to strengthen conformity, not individuality. It is basically at odds with our founding principles and any sensible approach to personal liberty.

It is a vacuous and demeaning exercise in nationalism, beneath the dignity of any democratically minded person.

The Pledge of Allegiance should be swiftly consigned to the burn pile along with any other public displays of loyalty to the Fatherland.

*"The removal of "under God" in the Pledge of Allegiance would represent a disastrous imposition of official secularism as the nation's public."*

# Removing the Phrase "Under God" in the Pledge of Allegiance Is an Attempt to Establish Secularism

## *Albert Mohler*

*Albert Mohler is president of the Southern Baptist Theological Seminary. In the following viewpoint, he contends that the phrase "under God" in the Pledge of Allegiance represents an acknowledgment of a higher power but does not impose that belief on others. Mohler views attacks on the phrase as a systematic attempt to impose a secularist belief on the religious majority and eliminate religious expression from the public sphere.*

As you read, consider the following questions:

1. How did the Ninth US Circuit Court of Appeals rule in 2002 on Michael Newdow's lawsuit, as cited by the author?

Albert Mohler, "Is the Pledge of Allegiance Unconstitutional?," AlbertMohler.com, September 15, 2005. Copyright © 2005 by The Southern Baptist Theological Seminary. Reproduced by permission.

2. Why did the US Supreme Court set aside the case in 2004, according to Mohler?

3. How does the author think that the US Supreme Court will rule on this new lawsuit?

A federal judge in Sacramento ruled Wednesday [September 14, 2005,] that it is unconstitutional to recite the Pledge of Allegiance in public schools. U.S. District Judge Lawrence Karlton ruled that the pledge's reference to one nation "under God" violates the right of children in the public schools to be "free from a coercive requirement to affirm God."

Once again, the driving force behind this case is Michael Newdow, an attorney and medical doctor who won a similar decision at the 9th U.S. Circuit Court of Appeals in 2002. That court ruled that Newdow, an atheist, had successfully made his case that requiring his daughter to recite the pledge of allegiance with the words "under God" violated his own first amendment freedoms. In essence, the California-based appeals court ruled that the mere presence of the words "under God" in the Pledge of Allegiance constituted an establishment of religion by the government.

The 2002 decision sent shockwaves across the country, but that decision was set aside last year [2004] by the U.S. Supreme Court. Nevertheless, the nation's High Court dismissed the case after ruling that Newdow lacked standing because he did not have custody of his daughter at the time the suit was filed. Given the Supreme Court's decision not to rule on the actual merits of Newdow's argument, the stage was set for a second round of litigation.

Newdow, the Energizer bunny of secular litigation, filed the current case on behalf of three unnamed parents who have children in the California public schools. Judge Karlton ruled that the unnamed families do have standing and are thus entitled to sue.

## Analyzing the Judge's Opinion

In the judge's thirty-page opinion, he identifies the first two parents as "Jan and Pat Doe," who are described as residents of Sacramento County who have a seventh grader in the Elk Grove United School District. The third plaintiff, identified as "Jan Roe," is the father of a third grade student enrolled in the Sacramento area public schools.

The judge's decision also includes a fascinating description of the plaintiffs and their children. The seventh grade son of Jan and Pat Doe is described as "an atheist who denies the existence of God." The parents are described in identical terms. According to the judge's findings, "They contend that Doe child has been forced to experience the recitation of the Pledge that has been led by public school teachers in class and at public assemblies. Plaintiff Doe child has suffered harassment by other students due to Doe child's refusal to participate in the Pledge."

The Roe child is identified as a third grade student who is "a pantheist, who denies the existence of a personal God." The judge's decision states: "She has been forced to experience the recitation of the Pledge of Allegiance in her classes and has been led by her teachers in her class and at assemblies in reciting the Pledge." A pantheist in the third grade?

The parents also allege that they individually have been "made to feel like a 'political outsider' due to the 'government's embrace of (Christian) monotheism in the Pledge of Allegiance.'" Further, "The parents contend that they are deeply involved in the education of their children, and that they have attempted to participate in school matters, but once their atheism becomes known, it interferes with their ability to 'fit in' and 'effect changes within the political climate of parent-teacher associations [and] school board meetings.'"

Newdow also "alleges that he is an atheist who denies the existence of any god." Furthermore, "Newdow avers that his child is forced to experience teacher-led recitation of the

Pledge of Allegiance every morning, even though he has requested the principal of his child's school and the [school district] that the practice be discontinued."

Judge Karlton cited the 2002 decision by the Ninth Circuit and reiterated its ruling that the schools' pledge policy "impermissibly coerces a religious act." Accordingly, he ruled that the schools' policy must be changed and announced that he would soon issue a stay ordering that the practice of reciting the pledge be halted in affected schools.

## Leaving It Up to the Supreme Court

Clearly, this case will soon make its way back to the Supreme Court. Given the circumstances, it is unlikely that the High Court will be able to dismiss the case on the technicality of standing. In all likelihood, the Court will decide finally to rule on the constitutionality of the Pledge with the words "under God" as inserted by Congress in 1954.

How will the Supreme Court rule? That answer is anything but certain. Given the High Court's recent pattern of rulings in church-state cases, observers are left with no definitive guide that would predict how it might rule in this case. If anything, the Court's rulings on the public display of the Ten Commandments in its last term did nothing but add to the confusion.

Interestingly, Judge Karlton expressed relief that, given his deference to the Ninth Circuit's previous ruling, he did not have to consider the Supreme Court's most recent decisions. He expressed his thinking in a footnote: "This court will be less than candid if it did not acknowledge that it is relieved that, by virtue of the disposition above, it need not attempt to apply the Supreme Court's recently articulated distinction between those governmental activities which endorse religion and are thus prohibited, and those which acknowledge the Nation's asserted religious heritage, and thus are permitted."

"Pledge of Allegiance," cartoon by Jeff Parker. Copyright © by Jeff Parker, *Florida Today*, and www.PoliticalCartoons.com. All rights reserved.

In other words, the judge confessed that he really did not know what the Supreme Court meant to say. He's in good company.

Without doubt, the Court has demonstrated an increasing hostility toward the public display of any theistic belief. In the Ten Commandments decisions—with a collection of opinions amounting to a mass of confusion—the justices indicated an inclination toward an increasingly subjective test. In essence, the outcome of any future case concerning the Pledge will have everything to do with the composition of the Court and the proclivities of the individual justices.

## Religious Expression Is Under Attack

What does all this mean? Christians should be careful to think clearly about the Pledge of Allegiance and the current controversy. Secularists like Michael Newdow represent the hard edge of ideological attacks upon all expressions of theistic belief in the public arena. The truth is that the courts have allowed and driven a constriction of religious liberty such that any public reference or acknowledgment of the beliefs common to vast millions of Americans is now considered to represent an unconstitutional establishment of religion by the government.

In recent years this has meant the eradication of prayers at public events such as graduation ceremonies and football games, and the removal of monuments and emblems from government property and vehicles.

All this puts believing Christians in a difficult position. After all, the Court has ruled that symbols and references to a divine being are allowable only insofar as those references point to no specific deity. Beyond this, the courts have ruled that the only permissible reference to deity is a reference that so reduces the definition of deity that it appears difficult for all but the most ardent atheist to object.

## The Meaning of the Phrase

Because of this, Christians must not defend the presence of the words "under God" in the Pledge as a direct reference to the God of Abraham, Isaac, and Jacob—the Triune God whom Christians worship as Father, Son, and Holy Spirit. At best, the presence of this language in the Pledge and similar expressions on the nation's currency represent an acknowledgement of a power higher than the State itself and the nation's dependency upon that power for its safety and well being. Nevertheless, a decision from the Supreme Court that would require the removal of "under God" in the Pledge of Allegiance would represent a disastrous imposition of official secularism as the nation's public commitment.

Michael Newdow and company will not be satisfied until the United States government is not only secular, but *secularist*. That's the real agenda behind his lawsuits and what is really at stake in any future rulings. To accept his argument at face value, one would have to believe that the United States of America has functioned as a theocracy of sorts for the last half century. A little sanity would go a long way in this case.

> *"The Dover Area School Board . . . decision . . . to insert intelligent design into the science curriculum violates the constitutional separation of church and state."*

# Teaching Intelligent Design Is a Violation of the Separation of Church and State

## *MSNBC.com*

*MSNBC.com is a news website. The following viewpoint chronicles the controversy over a Pennsylvania public school board decision to teach intelligent design in science classes in local schools and a federal judge's decision that the board was violating the separation of church and state by promoting religion in the classroom. US district judge John E. Jones concluded that Dover Area School Board members deceived parents and connived to misrepresent science and offer religious belief as scientific theory.*

As you read, consider the following questions:

1. According to the author, when did the Dover Area School Board decide to insert intelligent design into the science curriculum?

2. What is intelligent design, as described by MSNBC.com?

3. What was the Scopes Trial, as described by the author?

In one of the biggest courtroom clashes between faith and evolution since the 1925 Scopes Monkey Trial, a federal judge barred a Pennsylvania public school district [in December 2005] from teaching "intelligent design" in biology class, saying the concept is creationism in disguise.

U.S. District Judge John E. Jones delivered a stinging attack on the Dover Area School Board, saying its first-in-the-nation decision in October 2004 to insert intelligent design into the science curriculum violates the constitutional separation of church and state.

## A Setback for Creationists

The ruling was a major setback to the intelligent design movement, which is also waging battles in Georgia and Kansas. Intelligent design holds that living organisms are so complex that they must have been created by some kind of higher force.

Jones decried the "breathtaking inanity" of the Dover policy and accused several board members of lying to conceal their true motive, which he said was to promote religion.

A six-week trial over the issue yielded "overwhelming evidence" establishing that intelligent design "is a religious view, a mere re-labeling of creationism, and not a scientific theory," said Jones, a Republican and a churchgoer appointed to the federal bench [in 2002].

The school system said it will probably not appeal the ruling, because the members who backed intelligent design were ousted in November's elections and replaced with a new slate opposed to the policy.

## An Alternative to Evolution

During the trial, the board argued that it was trying improve science education by exposing students to alternatives to Charles Darwin's theory of evolution and natural selection.

The policy required students to hear a statement about intelligent design before ninth-grade lessons on evolution. The statement said Darwin's theory is "not a fact" and has inexplicable "gaps." It referred students to an intelligent-design textbook, *Of Pandas and People*.

But the judge said: "We find that the secular purposes claimed by the board amount to a pretext for the board's real purpose, which was to promote religion in the public school classroom."

The disclaimer, he said, "singles out the theory of evolution for special treatment, misrepresents its status in the scientific community, causes students to doubt its validity without scientific justification, presents students with a religious alternative masquerading as a scientific theory, directs them to consult a creationist text as though it were a science resource and instructs students to forgo scientific inquiry in the public school classroom and instead to seek out religious instruction elsewhere."

## Reactions to the Decision

In 1987, the U.S. Supreme Court ruled that states cannot require public schools to balance evolution lessons by teaching creationism.

Eric Rothschild, an attorney for the families who challenged the policy, called the ruling "a real vindication for the parents who had the courage to stand up and say there was something wrong in their school district."

Richard Thompson, president and chief counsel of the Thomas More Law Center in Ann Arbor, Mich., which represented the school district and describes its mission as defending the religious freedom of Christians, said: "What this really looks like is an ad hominem [personal] attack on scientists who happen to believe in God."

It was the latest chapter in a debate over the teaching of evolution dating back to the Scopes trial in which Tennessee

"Yeah, but I'm afraid those in favor of teaching 'intelligent design' never met my husband," cartoon by Marty Bucella, www.CartoonStock.com. Copyright © by Marty Bucella. Reproduction rights available from www.CartoonStock.com.

biology teacher John T. Scopes was fined $100 for violating a state law against teaching evolution.

## Recent Legal Clashes

Earlier this month [December 2005], a federal appeals court in Georgia heard arguments over whether a suburban Atlanta school district had the right to put stickers on biology textbooks describing evolution as a theory, not fact. A federal judge last January ordered the stickers removed.

In November, state education officials in Kansas adopted new classroom science standards that call the theory of evolution into question.

President [George W.] Bush also weighed in on the issue of intelligent design recently, saying schools should present the concept when teaching about the origins of life.

## Decision: Intelligent Design Is Not Science

In his ruling, Jones said that while intelligent design, or ID, arguments "may be true, a proposition on which the court takes no position, ID is not science." Among other things, he said intelligent design "violates the centuries-old ground rules of science by invoking and permitting supernatural causation"; it relies on "flawed and illogical" arguments; and its attacks on evolution "have been refuted by the scientific community."

"The students, parents, and teachers of the Dover Area School District deserved better than to be dragged into this legal maelstrom, with its resulting utter waste of monetary and personal resources," he wrote.

Jones wrote that he wasn't saying the intelligent design concept shouldn't be studied and discussed, saying its advocates "have bona fide and deeply held beliefs which drive their scholarly endeavors."

But, he wrote, "our conclusion today is that it is unconstitutional to teach ID as an alternative to evolution in a public school science classroom."

The judge also said: "It is ironic that several of these individuals, who so staunchly and proudly touted their religious convictions in public, would time and again lie to cover their tracks and disguise the real purpose behind the ID Policy."

Former school board member William Buckingham, who advanced the policy, said from his new home in Mount Airy, N.C., that he still feels the board did the right thing.

## "We Were Robbed"

"I'm still waiting for a judge or anyone to show me anywhere in the Constitution where there's a separation of church and state," he said. "We didn't lose; we were robbed."

The controversy divided Dover and surrounding Dover Township, a rural area of nearly 20,000 residents about 20 miles south of Harrisburg. It galvanized voters to oust eight school board members who supported the policy in the Nov. 8 [2004] school board election. The ninth board member was not up for re-election.

The new school board president, Bernadette Reinking, said the board intends to remove intelligent design from the science curriculum and place it in an elective social studies class.

"As far as I can tell you, there is no intent to appeal," she said.

The old board's actions may still have an impact, however. Jones also ruled that the school board would have to pay the plaintiffs' legal fees, which are not insignificant.

> *"The U.S. Constitution guarantees that nondiscriminatory teaching of Creation Science and Intelligent Design Theory and freedom of speech cannot be denied to schools. "*

# Teaching Intelligent Design Is Not a Violation of the Separation of Church and State

*Jack Wellman*

*Jack Wellman is a Christian author of several books. In the following viewpoint, he points to a 1987 Supreme Court decision that refers to intelligent design as science to reinforce the idea that it is a legitimate scientific theory that should be taught in schools. Wellman contends that preventing school districts from teaching intelligent design if that is what they want to do violates their right to free speech and imposes a secularist view on the majority.*

As you read, consider the following questions:

1. According to the author, what did Thomas Jefferson mean when he penned the phrase "separation of church and state"?

2. What is Louisiana's Creationism Act, as described by Wellman?

3. How does the author interpret the *Edwards v. Aguillard* Supreme Court decision?

Where do you find the Separation of Church and State? In the U.S. Constitution? In the Articles? In the Amendments? How about in the Declaration of Independence? You will not find it in any legal document in the United States. This phrase, penned by Thomas Jefferson was for a wall of separation between church and state, because in England, the State was the Church. It was a church-state. This is what inspired Jefferson in his memoirs, that simply a division of labor be established. That's all he meant. The government shouldn't fund religion or impose it at the state level as compulsory. Nor could the State impose it's ideology upon the churches.

Suppose that a flat-Earth religion became very popular and books appeared defending the flat-Earth hypothesis. Flat-Earth parents, of course, would be very unhappy to find that the public schools were teaching a round Earth. Some of them would move their children into private schools that taught flat-Earth theory. Others would campaign against the "brainwashing" of their children in the public schools. They might demand equal time for their flat-Earth views. How would you handle that potato? It would be irresponsible, of course, for you to allow the flat-Earth view into the geography curriculum. Time spent on the evidences for a flat-Earth is time robbed from serious learning.

The Supreme Court has already made it crystal clear that the teaching of creation science cannot be legally prohibited from being taught in the classroom, if the local school district opts for it. Incidentally, this is what the Supreme Court calls it: Creation-science. Chief Justice [William] Rehnquist & Justice [Antonin] Scalia, "We have no basis on the record to conclude that creation-science need be anything other than a collection of scientific data supporting the theory that life abruptly appeared on the earth." *Edwards vs. Aguillard*, Dissent (1987).

The meaning of the First Amendment of the U.S. Constitution should be disbarred. This Amendment clearly says, "Congress cannot pass any law concerning a religion or establishing a religion; and cannot pass any law that prevents the free exercise of religion." To do otherwise is clearly a violation of the Constitution and discrimination and hate crime against believers. The U.S. Supreme Court decision concerning separation of church and state is clearly a violation of the U.S. Constitution.

Louisiana's "Creationism Act" The *Edwards v. Aguillard*— Supreme Court Decision, forbade the teaching of the theory of evolution in public elementary and secondary schools unless accompanied by instruction in the theory of creation science. Appellees, who include Louisiana parents, teachers, and religious leaders, challenged the Act's constitutionality in Federal District Court, seeking an injunction and declaratory relief. The District Court granted summary judgment to Appellees, holding that the Act violated the Establishment Clause of the First Amendment. The Court of Appeals affirmed (http://www.nwcreation.net/trials.html).

The U.S. Constitution guarantees that nondiscriminatory teaching of Creation Science and Intelligent Design Theory and freedom of speech cannot be denied to schools. The power to legislate—pass laws is specifically allocated in the U.S. Constitution to Congress; not the U.S. Supreme Court justices.

What laws Congress cannot make are also stated in the Constitution. The Supreme Court is the judicial branch of our government, conceived as a counterbalance to the legislative branch. In this capacity it has the ability not to make laws, but to judge whether or not a law is being broken. The courts have been making laws, and this is not their job. That falls to Congress and then to two thirds majority of the states.

The legal challenges to Intelligent Design center around the notion that if a superior being created the universe and that superior being is God—then such a theory violates the separation of church and state and cannot be taught in public schools. But consider what the Supreme Court has said about this issue. In 1987, in *Edwards v. Aguillard*, the high court concluded that "teaching a variety of scientific theories about the origins of humankind to school children might be validly done with the clear secular intent of enhancing the effectiveness of science instruction." The court also said that teaching these theories would pose no constitutional problems provided they are not taught to the exclusion of evolution. If the classroom is indeed, as the Supreme Court has said, "the marketplace of ideas," why not teach multiple theories regarding the origins of mankind—including Intelligent Design?

Parents and their children ought to have the right to question current theories and be able to consider alternative explanations, especially when a theory is regarded as fact and has yet to be conclusively proven. Let the children make up their own minds. What do evolutionists have to fear? Evolution has become like a state ideology and instead of people worrying about the separation of church and state, it has turned to an effort to become a separation of church from state. This was most certainly not the founding fathers intent. And intent is everything.

# Periodical and Internet Sources Bibliography

*The following articles have been selected to supplement the diverse views presented in this chapter.*

Adelle M. Banks — "Retired Chaplains Oppose Don't Ask/Don't Tell Repeal," *HuffingtonPost*, April 29, 2010.

Kambiz Ghanea Bassiri — "Religion Dispatches: Is Religious Freedom a Casualty at Ground Zero?," Council on Foreign Relations, August 10, 2010. www.cfr.org.

David Limbaugh — "Ground Zero Mosque Reveals Left's Hypocrisy on Religion," Newsmax.com, August 20, 2010. www.newsmax.com.

Audrey Love — "Don't Ask Don't Tell Policy Essential to Nation," *Reflector*, September 30, 2010.

Barry Lynn — "Opposition to DADT Is About Religion," *Washington Post*, November 16, 2010.

E. Thomas McClanahan — "Building a Mosque at Ground Zero Is Distasteful," *Kansas City (MO) Star*, August 14, 2010.

Terry Newell — "Ground Zero Mosque Opposition: Shall We Retreat from Religious Freedom?," *HuffingtonPost*, August 2, 2010.

Tony Perkins — "My Take: Ending 'Don't Ask, Don't Tell' Would Undermine Religious Liberty," CNN.com, June 1, 2010. www.cnn.com.

Staks Rosch — "On Faith: DADT, Religion Won't Compromise," *Philadelphia Examiner*, November 16, 2010.

Jack A. Smith — "The Muslim Mosque at Ground Zero and Freedom of Religion in America," *Global Research*, August 27, 2010.

# For Further Discussion

## Chapter 1

1. During the past few years, there have been a number of public and religious figures who argue that the "wall" between Church and State was not rooted in the First Amendment. After reading the viewpoints by Charles C. Haynes and Ken Klukowski, give your interpretation of the establishment clause, applying it to the principle of church-state separation.

2. In his viewpoint, Robert Knight contends that America is a Christian nation. Stuart Whatley counters with his belief that America is based on secular notions. After reading both viewpoints, what is your opinion? How do your own views on religion influence your answer?

3. Has the separation of church and state gone too far in contemporary America, or is religious expression too public? Cite from the viewpoints by Barry Lynn and Louis DeBroux to inform your answer.

4. Elizabeth Katz asserts that the separation of church and state was meant to protect religious liberty from government intervention. Christopher Merola, however, argues that it hinders religious liberty by curtailing religious expression. Which argument do you think is more persuasive and why?

## Chapter 2

1. Should religious leaders get involved in politics? Cite from the viewpoints by Ronald J. Rychlak and Lisa Fabrizio to inform your answer.

2. David Limbaugh believes that it is inevitable that a politician's religious beliefs will influence his or her policy

making. In his viewpoint, Jeffrey S. Victor argues that policy makers should put their religious beliefs aside in order to make good policy. Which do you feel is a more accurate perspective on religion and politics? Use examples to support your opinion.

## Chapter 3

1. The immigration debate has been one of the most controversial issues of the past few years. Cindy Carcamo asserts that many religious leaders are becoming more and more active regarding the issue. Benjamin Van Horrick argues that such activism is an act of political convenience for both the church and politicians. How active should religious leaders be in the debate? Explain your answer.

2. In his viewpoint, James Brosnahan contends that Proposition 8 in California violates the separation of church and state. Robert Alt argues that it does not violate the principle of church-state separation. After reading both viewpoints, what are your beliefs on the issue? Do your religious views inform your opinion? Why or why not?

3. Should taxpayers be forced to fund government actions that are against their religious beliefs? Cite from the viewpoints on the issue of embryonic stem cell research by Warren Mass and David Holcberg and Alex Epstein to inform your answer.

4. Since it passed in 1996, the Defense of Marriage Act (DOMA) has proven to be very controversial. Ron Sider thinks that repealing DOMA will threaten religious freedom. Geoffrey R. Stone asserts that it is unconstitutional and has to be repealed. After reading both viewpoints, which author do you think makes a more persuasive argument? Why?

# Chapter 4

1. The Cordoba House Project, otherwise known as Park51 or the Ground Zero Mosque, has a lot of critics, including George Neumayr, calling for the project to be banned. Katha Pollitt argues that banning the community center would be a violation of the separation of church and state. After reading both viewpoints, what do you see as the answer to this controversy?

2. The debate about repealing the "Don't Ask, Don't Tell" policy regarding gays serving in the military led to concerns that military chaplains would be forced to compromise their religious beliefs on homosexuality if the policy were repealed. After reading the viewpoints by Daniel Blomberg and Gene Robinson, do you think this is a valid concern? Why or why not?

# Organizations to Contact

*The editors have compiled the following list of organizations concerned with the issues debated in this book. The descriptions are derived from materials provided by the organizations. All have publications or information available for interested readers. The list was compiled on the date of publication of the present volume; the information provided here may change. Be aware that many organizations take several weeks or longer to respond to inquiries, so allow as much time as possible.*

## Alliance Defense Fund (ADF)

15100 N. Ninetieth St., Scottsdale, AZ   85260
(800) 835-5233 • fax: (480) 444-0028
website: www.alliancedefensefund.org

The Alliance Defense Fund is a Christian legal organization that defends religious freedom and fights against same-sex marriage and abortion rights. Established in 1994 by American evangelical leaders, ADF trains Christian attorneys, coordinates with other evangelical groups to advance Christian causes, and litigates cases that correspond to Christian beliefs. The ADF website offers pamphlets, videos, and books on issues such as freedom of religious expression in the workplace or same-sex marriage, and the site features a blog that explores issues in the news and updates on current legal cases. The website also links to press releases, audio presentations, and ADF responses to media stories and commentary.

## American Civil Liberties Union (ACLU)

125 Broad St., 18th Fl., New York, NY   10004
(888) 567-2258
website: www.aclu.org

The American Civil Liberties Union is a national organization that works to protect the rights of individuals and communities as prescribed by the US Constitution. The ACLU lobbies

Congress to pass legislation protecting civil liberties; employs lawyers to fight discrimination and injustice in court; and organizes activists, volunteers, and other organizations to protest the violation of civil liberties. The ACLU website features a blog, called *The Blog of Rights,* that offers opinions and commentary from ACLU staff and legal scholars on hot topics and current campaigns and cases. The website also provides video of interviews, commentary, and presentations on ACLU efforts on subjects such as Don't Ask Don't Tell (DADT), immigration, and same-sex marriage.

## Americans United for the Separation of Church and State (AU)

518 C St. NE, Washington, DC   20002
(202) 466-3234 • fax: (202) 466-2587
e-mail: americansunited@au.org
website: www.au.org

Americans United for the Separation of Church and State is an educational nonprofit organization that works to secure and protect the principle of church-state separation. AU is active in a number of issues, such as school vouchers, faith-based initiatives, religion in public schools, religious expression in the public arena, and church politicking. It also brings lawsuits and provides legal counsel with the goal of strengthening the wall of separation between church and state. The AU website features a blog, a calendar of events, alerts on pressing issues, and videos of congressional testimony, interesting speeches, and television appearances by AU members. The website also offers information on AU books, brochures, reports, research, and court decisions.

## Campaign for Liberty

5211 Port Royal Rd., Ste. 310, Springfield, VA   22151
(703) 865-7162 • fax: (703) 865-7549
website: www.campaignforliberty.com

The Campaign for Liberty is a conservative membership organization that strives to promote and defend the great American principles of individual liberty, constitutional government, sound money, free markets, and a noninterventionist foreign policy by means of educational and political activity. It is one of the main sponsors of the Conservative Political Action Conference (CPAC), an influential meeting for conservative activists, and the grassroots leadership schools, which train the next generation of conservative leaders and activists. The Campaign for Liberty website has a section of educational material, including bibliographies for prospective members.

**Center for Individual Rights (CIR)**
1233 Twentieth St. NW, Ste. 300, Washington, DC   20036
(202) 833-8400 • fax: (202) 833-8410
website: www.cir-usa.org

The Center for Individual Rights is a nonprofit public law firm that works to defend individual liberties against the growth of the federal government's power. CIR litigates cases that enforce constitutional limits on state and federal governments, such as excessive regulation, free speech issues, and civil liberties. The CIR website offers information on active and settled cases as well as updates on events and relevant legal issues. The organization also publishes a newsletter, *CIR Docket Reports*, that examines newsmakers, events, and controversies that involve CIR cases.

**First Amendment Center**
1207 Eighteenth Ave. South, Nashville, TN   37212
(615) 727-1600 • fax: (615) 727-1319
e-mail: info@fac.org
website: www.firstamendmentcenter.org/

The First Amendment Center is a nonpartisan educational and research group located at Vanderbilt University with offices also in Washington, DC. Its main mission is to support the First Amendment to the US Constitution through the media, education, and advocacy. The First Amendment Center's website publishes a weekly column, Inside the First Amendment, that provides timely and thought-provoking commentary on First Amendment issues in the news. The website also features *First Reports*, a series of in-depth analyses, and *State of the First Amendment*, a periodic survey of American attitudes on First Amendment issues. The First Amendment Center also sponsors seminars, lectures, educational programs, and Freedom Sings, a multimedia presentation and concert that has an annual tour.

**Freedom from Religion Foundation (FFRF)**
PO Box 750, Madison, WI  53701
(608) 256-8900 • fax: (608) 204-0422
website: www.ffrf.org

The Freedom from Religion Foundation is a nonprofit educational group committed to strengthening the separation of church and state and to disseminating information about nontheism. Since its founding in 1978, FFRF has addressed complaints and initiated key lawsuits to clarify and reinforce the principle of church and state separation. FFRF publishes *Freethought Today*, a newspaper that covers FFRF action and news of interest, a blog that examines relevant topics, educational brochures, action alerts, and fact sheets. The FFRF website has an online bookstore, which offers books, studies, and other publications for sale. FFRF sponsors events such as seminars, discussion groups, lectures, and a national convention.

**Institute on Religion and Public Policy**
500 N. Washington St., Alexandria, VA  22314
(703) 888-1700 • fax: (703) 888-1704
website: www.religionandpolicy.org

The Institute on Religion and Public Policy is an international nonpartisan organization that works to protect the practice of religious freedom around the world. To that end, it researches and disseminates information and analysis on oppressive governments and policies that threaten that freedom. The institute also sponsors programs and events to educate and motivate activists, government policy makers, academics, business executives, religious leaders, and nongovernmental organizations. It publishes a weekly newsletter, *Face of Freedom*, that offers analysis on the state of global religious freedom. In addition, the institute's website also features a blog that focuses on current issues and events.

**People for the American Way (PFAW)**
2000 M St. NW, Ste. 400, Washington, DC 20036
(202) 467-4999
website: www.pfaw.org

People for the American Way is a nonprofit progressive advocacy group. It describes its mission as being dedicated to making the promise of America real for every American: Equality. Freedom of speech. Freedom of religion. The right to seek justice in a court of law. The right to cast a vote that counts. The American Way. PFAW is particularly active in issues that involve the separation of church and state. The PFAW website features three blogs: one that concentrates on youth issues, one that monitors the right-wing media, and one that explores topical issues. The organization's website also links to recent television appearances by PFAW officials, audio clips and interviews, featured reports and studies, and press releases.

**Secular Coalition for America**
PO Box 66096, Washington, DC 20035
(202) 299-1091
website: www.secular.org

The Secular Coalition for America is a nonprofit advocacy organization that brings together several organizations that are committed to promoting the voices and interests of the nontheistic (atheists and agnostics) in the United States. One of its biggest priorities is protecting the secular character of the US government by strengthening the wall between church and state. The organization's website features press releases, congressional scorecards, action alerts, and fact sheets on recent issues of interest to members.

# Bibliography of Books

Robert Audi      *Democratic Authority and the Separation of Church and State.* New York: Oxford University Press, 2011.

Hunter Baker      *The End of Secularism.* Wheaton, IL: Crossway Books, 2009.

Patrick McKinley Brennan      *Civilizing Authority: Society, State, and Church.* Lanham, MD: Lexington Books, 2007.

William T. Cavanaugh      *Migrations of the Holy: God, State, and the Political Meaning of the Church.* Grand Rapids, MI: W.B. Eerdmans, 2011.

Erwin Chemerinsky      *The Conservative Assault on the Constitution.* New York: Simon & Schuster, 2010.

Forrest Church      *So Help Me God: The Founding Fathers and the First Great Battle over Church and State.* Orlando, FL: Harcourt, 2007.

John J. DiIulio Jr.      *Godly Republic: A Centrist Civic Blueprint for America's Faith-Based Future.* Berkeley and Los Angeles: University of California Press, 2007.

Donald L. Drakeman      *Church, State, and Original Intent.* New York: Cambridge University Press, 2010.

Robert Fatton Jr. and R.K. Ramazani, eds. *Religion, State, and Society: Jefferson's Wall of Separation in Comparative Perspective.* New York: Palgrave Macmillan, 2009.

Jerald Finney *Separation of Church and State: God's Churches, Spiritual or Legal Entities?* Austin, TX: Kerygma, 2009.

C. Welton Gaddy and Barry W. Lynn *First Freedom First: A Citizen's Guide to Protecting Religious Liberty and the Separation of Church and State.* Boston: Beacon, 2008.

James H. Hutson *Church and State in America: The First Two Centuries.* Cambridge: Cambridge University Press, 2008.

Ted J. Jelen *To Serve God and Mammon: Church-State Relations in American Politics.* Washington, DC: Georgetown University Press, 2010.

Sandra F. Joireman, ed. *Church, State, and Citizen: Christian Approaches to Political Engagement.* New York: Oxford University Press, 2009.

P.C. Kemeny *Church, State, and Public Justice: Five Views.* Downers Grove, IL: InterVarsity Press, 2007.

Damon Linker *The Religious Test: Why We Must Question the Beliefs of Our Leaders.* New York: Norton, 2010.

Scott A. Merriman — *Religion and the State: An International Analysis of Roles and Relationships.* Santa Barbara, CA: ABC-CLIO, 2009.

Stephen V. Monsma and J. Christopher Soper — *The Challenge of Pluralism: Church and State in Five Democracies.* Lanham, MD: Rowman & Littlefield, 2009.

Vincent Philip Muñoz — *God and the Founders: Madison, Washington, and Jefferson.* New York: Cambridge University Press, 2009.

Monica Najar — *Evangelizing the South: A Social History of Church and State in Early America.* New York: Oxford University Press, 2008.

Michael Leo Owens — *God and Government in the Ghetto: The Politics of Church-State Collaboration in Black America.* Chicago: University of Chicago Press, 2007.

Tara Ross and Joseph C. Smith Jr. — *Under God: George Washington and the Question of Church and State.* Dallas: Spence, 2008.

Steven H. Shiffrin — *The Religious Left and Church-State Relations.* Princeton, NJ: Princeton University Press, 2009.

Stephen D. Solomon — *Ellery's Protest: How One Young Man Defied Tradition & Sparked the Battle over School Prayer.* Ann Arbor: The University of Michigan Press, 2007.

J. Brent Walker    *Church-State Matters: Fighting for Religious Liberty in Our Nation's Capital.* Macon, GA: Mercer University Press, 2008.

Jeffrey S. Walz and Steven R. Montreal    *Lutheran Pastors and Politics: Issues in the Public Square.* St. Louis, MO: Concordia, 2007.

# Index

## A

Abortion issues
    attempts at quieting priests, 75–76
    bombings of clinics, 94
    call for principled approach, 98
    Catholic doctrine, 119
    as consequence of freedom, 53
    distortions of, 99
    Hillary Clinton's viewpoint, 118
    Huckabee's view on, 87
    liberal viewpoint, 117
    partial-birth abortion, 129, 193
    pro-/antiabortionist values, 86
Adams, John, 56, 198
Adults in America, religious affiliations (chart), 35
Agnosticism, 37–38, 51, 91–92, 184, 198
Akridge, William, 192
Alito, Sam, 119
Alt, Robert, 126–130
Alzheimer's disease, 134
American Civil Liberties Union (ACLU), 50–51, 177, 182
Americans United for Life, 95
Appleby, Kevin, 114
Aquinas, Thomas, 38
Aristotle, 41
Arizona, immigration rulings, 70–71
Ashcroft, John, 199

Atheism, 37–38, 45, 51, 62, 86, 91–92, 198

## B

Barnes, Melody C., 137
Barton, David, 32, 33
Bea, Carlos, 62
Beck, Glenn, 32, 33
Benitez, Roger T., 64–65
Bible
    abortion/gay rights positions, 118
    anti-choice activism issue, 45
    Hebrew Bible and Moses, 34
    property rights endorsements, 35–36
    religious choice, school prayer, 67
    teachings on compassion, 111
Biden, Joe, 74
Bill of Rights, 24
Black, Hugo, 61
Blomberg, Daniel, 191–195
Bloomberg, Michael, 16, 176, 180
Bob Jones University, 155
Boykin, William, 199
Brewer, Jan, 70
Brogio, Timothy, 173
Brosnahan, James, 121–125
Brownback, Sam, 74
Buddhists, 36, 85
Bunch, Will, 32, 33, 35
Bush, George W.
    alignment with religious fanatics, 199
    anti-stem cell stance, 112, 137

Axis of Evil statement, 184
intelligent design comments, 212
"messianic militarist" label, 88

**C**

California
black-white marriage ruling, 123–124
church immigrant activism, 111, 114
Poway United School District, 63–64
suspension of indecency laws, 52
University Jewish Synagogue, 112
*See also* Proposition 8
California Supreme Court, 122–123, 127–129
Calvin, John, 41
Camarota, Steven, 113
Candidates (political candidates)
Catholic presidential candidates, 74
excess reliance on religion, 101–104
pragmatism and principle, 97–98
promoting for the common good, 97
qualifications vs. religious background, 104–105
religious beliefs expressed by, 95–100
role of religion, 98–100
substance vs. style, 96–97
voter concerns about, 104
voting for virtues, 97

*See also* Huckabee, Mike; Politics in America; Romney, Mitt
Cantor, Eric, 138
Carcamo, Cindy, 110–115
Catholic Adoption Services, 50
*Catholic New York* newspaper, 148
*Catholic World Report*, 75
Catholicism (and Catholic Church), 25, 40–41
ancient Rome, 40–41
antireligious people vs., 79
bishop-priest shifts in power, 77
Democratic Party criticisms, 119
Diocese of Bridgeport (CT), 78–83
government funding for, 46
immigration activism, 117–120
Kennedy's statement about his religion, 105
problems of Catholic schools, 148–149
Protestant attacks on Catholics, 25–26
support for Proposition 8, 108
vouchers/faith-based schools, 145
*See also* Pfleger, Father Michael
Center for a Just Society, 95
Center for American Progress, 112
Center for Immigration Studies, 113
Center for Legal and Judicial Studies, 126
Chavez, Hugo, 47
Children's Hospital (Boston), 139